D0295119

mince

100 everyday recipes

First published in 2012
LOVE FOOD is an imprint of Parragon Books Ltd

Parragon
Queen Street House
4 Queen Street
Bath BA1 1HE, UK

Copyright © Parragon Books Ltd 2012

LOVE FOOD and the accompanying heart device is a registered trade mark of Parragon Books Ltd in Australia, the UK, USA, India and the EU.

www.parragon.com/lovefood

All rights reserved. No part of this publication may be reproduced, stored in a retrieval system, or transmitted, in any form or by any means, electronic, mechanical, photocopying, recording, or otherwise, without the prior permission of the copyright holder.

ISBN: 978-1-4454-9873-7

Printed in China

Produced by Ivy Contract
Cover and new photography by Clive Bozzard-Hill
Cover and new home economy and food styling by Mitzie Wilson

Notes for the Reader

This book uses both metric and imperial measurements. Follow the same units of measurement throughout; do not mix metric and imperial. All spoon measurements are level: teaspoons are assumed to be 5 ml, and tablespoons are assumed to be 15 ml. Unless otherwise stated, milk is assumed to be full fat, eggs and individual vegetables are medium, and pepper is freshly ground black pepper. Unless otherwise stated, all root vegetables should be washed in plain water and peeled prior to using.

For best results, use a food thermometer when cooking meat and poultry – check the latest government guidelines for current advice.

Garnishes, decorations and serving suggestions are all optional and not necessarily included in the recipe ingredients or method.

The times given are an approximate guide only. Preparation times differ according to the techniques used by different people and the cooking times may also vary from those given. Optional ingredients, variations or serving suggestions have not been included in the time calculations.

Recipes using raw or very lightly cooked eggs should be avoided by infants, the elderly, pregnant women, convalescents and anyone suffering from an illness. Pregnant and breastfeeding women are advised to avoid eating peanuts and peanut products. Sufferers from nut allergies should be aware that some of the ready-made ingredients used in the recipes in this book may contain nuts. Always check the packaging before use.

mince

introduction

Mince is one of the most widely used ingredients in modern cooking. It's the easiest, quickest meat you can cook with; a great and economical way to feed family and friends. It's a simple, wholesome and nutritious staple that freezes well and can be on the table in minutes when required. Mince tastes wonderful, and is actually something that nearly everyone likes!

Mince is endlessly versatile, and all kinds of meat can be minced, so it never gets boring. As well as being a source of protein, mince is an important source of iron, zinc and vitamin B12. Although leaner mince is more expensive, it contains less saturated fat and less weight will be lost in cooking (from fat and water). If you use mince that contains a lot of fat, dry-fry in a non-stick pan and then drain off the excess.

This book celebrates minced meat in all its forms. These 100 easy recipes include all our comfort food favourites, such as spaghetti Bolognese, chilli con carne, meatballs and moussaka. There are also recipes with a spicy spin, from Moroccan mince to curry and burritos, plus a whole range of burgers and kebabs,

from the classic to the gourmet. Many dishes can be made ahead and reheated when you need them, making them the ideal solution for family mid-week suppers or when entertaining.

Minced meat has always been popular, but most people have a rather limited repertoire of recipes. There's so much more to mince than cottage pie, and this book contains a range of delicious and inventive dishes that you may never have thought could be made from mince, such as dim sum, chicken, prosciutto and sun-dried tomato polpettini, Spanish rice, and turkey and chorizo empanadas. It is divided into chapters for rice and pasta dishes, burgers and kebabs, bakes and casseroles, spicy mince dishes, and small bites and nibbles. Within them you will find a wide selection of traditional and international recipes for all tastes and suitable for all occasions. From light lunch dishes to more impressive meals, this book will inspire you to try something a bit different, and provide you with the confidence to create a mince dish that is something really special.

rice & pasta dishes

spanish rice

ingredients

serves 4

1½ tbsp olive oil
1 onion, finely chopped
2 garlic cloves, finely chopped
1 red pepper, deseeded and
    finely chopped
85 g/3 oz chorizo sausage,
    chopped
250 g/9 oz fresh turkey mince
250 g/9 oz basmati rice
400 g/14 oz canned chopped
    tomatoes
pinch of saffron, infused in a little
    lukewarm water
700 ml/1¼ pints chicken stock
150 g/5½ oz frozen peas
salt and pepper

method

1 Heat the oil in a large, shallow saucepan. Add the onion, garlic, red pepper and chorizo and cook for 3–4 minutes.

2 Add the mince and continue to cook for 2–3 minutes, using a wooden spoon to break up the meat. Stir in the rice, tomatoes, infused saffron water, stock, and salt and pepper to taste.

3 Cover and cook for 15–18 minutes, until the rice is tender. Stir in the peas and cook for 1–2 minutes, until heated through. Serve immediately.

moroccan rice

ingredients

serves 4

500 g/1 lb 2 oz fresh beef mince
1 onion, finely chopped
1 garlic clove, finely chopped
1 tsp cumin seeds
1 tsp ground cinnamon
2 tsp ground turmeric
100 g/3½ oz ready-to-eat dried
    apricots, roughly chopped
50 g/1¾ oz raisins
225 g/8 oz basmati rice
600 ml/1 pint beef stock
salt and pepper
2 tbsp finely chopped fresh
    flat-leaf parsley and 2 tbsp
    toasted pine kernels, to garnish

method

1 Dry-fry the mince in a non-stick frying pan for
  4–5 minutes, until starting to brown. Add the onion
  and garlic and cook for a further 1–2 minutes.

2 Add the cumin seeds, cinnamon and turmeric and
  cook for 1–2 minutes, stirring constantly.

3 Add the apricots, raisins, rice and stock and season
  to taste with salt and pepper. Cover and cook for
  15–18 minutes, until the rice is tender.

4 Scatter over the parsley and pine kernels and serve
  the dish immediately.

beef pilau

ingredients

serves 4–6

125 ml/4 fl oz olive oil
3 onions, finely chopped
3 garlic cloves, finely chopped
800 g/1 lb 12 oz long-grain rice
1 tsp ground cumin
1 tsp ground turmeric
1 tsp ground coriander
1.7 litres/3 pints beef stock
600 g/1 lb 5 oz fresh
    beef mince
pinch of ground mace
1 tsp cumin seeds
2 tbsp chopped fresh mint
115 g/4 oz butter
salt and pepper
fresh coriander sprigs,
    to garnish

method

1 Heat 3 tablespoons of the oil in a saucepan. Add two-thirds of the onions and two-thirds of the garlic and cook over a low heat, stirring occasionally, for 5 minutes, until softened. Add the rice, ground cumin, turmeric and coriander and cook, stirring constantly, for 1 minute. Pour in the stock and bring to the boil. Stir well, reduce the heat, cover and simmer for 15–20 minutes, until the rice is tender and the liquid has been absorbed.

2 Meanwhile, put the remaining onion, remaining garlic, the beef, mace, cumin seeds and mint into a bowl. Season to taste with salt and pepper and mix well with your hands until thoroughly combined. Shape into walnut-sized balls.

3 Heat the remaining oil in a frying pan. Add the meatballs and cook over a medium heat, turning occasionally, for 6–8 minutes, until evenly browned and cooked through. Remove from the pan and drain on kitchen paper.

4 Remove the rice mixture from the heat and stir in the butter, then gently stir in the meatballs. Transfer to a warmed serving dish, garnish with coriander sprigs and serve immediately.

beef & pumpkin baked with rice

ingredients
serves 4

1 onion, finely chopped
500 g/1 lb 2 oz fresh beef
    mince
1 tbsp finely chopped fresh mint
½ tsp ground cinnamon
175 g/6 oz butter, plus extra
    for greasing
225 g/8 oz long-grain rice
500 g/1 lb 2 oz pumpkin or
    squash, peeled, deseeded
    and cut into cubes
2 tbsp brown sugar
salt and pepper

method

1 Put the onion, beef, mint and cinnamon into a bowl, season to taste with salt and pepper and mix well until thoroughly combined. Divide the mixture into eight equal portions and shape into small patties.

2 Melt 55 g/2 oz of the butter in a frying pan. Add the patties, in batches if necessary, and cook for 3–4 minutes on each side, until lightly browned. Remove with a fish slice.

3 Preheat the oven to 190°C/375°F/Gas Mark 5. Grease a large casserole with butter. Cook the rice in a large saucepan of salted boiling water for 15–20 minutes, until tender. Drain well and rinse with boiling water.

4 Spoon half the rice into the prepared casserole. Melt the remaining butter and pour half of it over the rice. Put the beef patties on top and cover with the remaining rice. Spread the pumpkin cubes over the top, sprinkle with the sugar and pour over the remaining melted butter. Cover and bake in the preheated oven for 25–30 minutes, until the pumpkin is tender. Serve immediately.

beef fried rice

ingredients

serves 6

500 g/1 lb 2 oz long-grain rice
2 tbsp groundnut oil
4 large eggs, lightly beaten
650 g/1 lb 7 oz
    fresh beef mince
1 large onion, finely chopped
2 garlic cloves, finely chopped
140 g/5 oz frozen peas
3 tbsp light soy sauce
1 tsp sugar
salt
prawn crackers, to serve

method

1 Cook the rice in a large saucepan of salted boiling water for 15 minutes, until tender. Drain the rice, rinse with boiling water and set aside.

2 Heat a wok over a medium heat, then add the groundnut oil, swirl it around the wok and heat. Add the eggs and cook, stirring constantly, for 50–60 seconds, until set. Transfer to a dish and set aside.

3 Add the beef to the wok and stir-fry, breaking it up with a wooden spoon, for 4–5 minutes, until evenly browned. Stir in the onion, garlic and peas and stir-fry for a further 3–4 minutes.

4 Add the rice, soy sauce, sugar and eggs and cook, stirring constantly, for a further 1–2 minutes, until heated through. Serve the stir-fry immediately with prawn crackers.

minced beef stroganoff

ingredients

serves 4

3 tbsp sunflower oil
1 onion, chopped
2 garlic cloves, finely chopped
225 g/8 oz mushrooms, sliced
500 g/1 lb 2 oz
    fresh beef mince
2 tbsp brandy
150 ml/5 fl oz beef stock
150 ml/5 fl oz soured cream
2 tbsp chopped fresh parsley,
    plus extra to garnish
salt and pepper

method

1 Heat 2 tablespoons of the oil in a large frying pan. Add the onion and garlic and cook over a low heat, stirring occasionally, for 5 minutes, until softened. Add the mushrooms and cook, stirring frequently, for a further 5 minutes. Using a slotted spoon, transfer the vegetables to a plate.

2 Add the remaining oil to the pan, then add the beef and cook over a medium heat, stirring frequently and breaking it up with a wooden spoon, for 5–8 minutes, until evenly browned. Drain off as much fat as possible.

3 Reduce the heat to low, return the vegetables to the pan and stir in the brandy. Cook, stirring occasionally, for 4–5 minutes, until the alcohol has evaporated. Stir in the stock, season to taste with salt and pepper and simmer gently, stirring frequently, for 15 minutes.

4 Stir in the soured cream and parsley and cook for a further minute. Garnish with parsley and serve the stroganoff immediately.

chicken, prosciutto & sun-dried tomato polpettini

ingredients

serves 4–6

500 g/1 lb 2 oz fresh chicken mince

50 g/1¾ oz prosciutto, roughly chopped

3 tbsp finely chopped fresh flat-leaf parsley

1 egg, beaten

85 g/3 oz fresh breadcrumbs

1 onion, finely chopped

50 g/1¾ oz sun-dried tomatoes, finely chopped

2–3 tbsp vegetable oil

salt and pepper

tomato sauce and cooked pasta, to serve

method

1 Put the mince, prosciutto, parsley, egg, breadcrumbs, onion, tomatoes, and salt and pepper to taste into a large bowl and mix with your fingertips to combine.

2 Shape the mixture into about 30 small balls, place on a baking tray and chill for 30 minutes.

3 Heat half the oil in a large, non-stick frying pan, add half the meatballs and cook for 15–20 minutes, turning regularly until the chicken is thoroughly cooked. Drain the meatballs on kitchen paper. Repeat with the remaining oil and meatballs.

4 Add to a hot tomato sauce and serve with pasta.

turkey tetrazzini

ingredients

serves 4

2 tbsp vegetable oil
500 g/1 lb 2 oz fresh turkey mince
1 onion, finely chopped
1 garlic clove, finely chopped
2 celery sticks, finely chopped
200 g/7 oz button mushrooms,
    finely sliced
2 tbsp plain flour
250 ml/9 fl oz chicken stock
4 tbsp single cream
3–4 drops Worcestershire sauce
125 g/4½ oz frozen peas
200 g/7 oz cooked spaghetti
4 tbsp freshly grated
    Parmesan cheese
salt and pepper

method

1 Preheat the oven to 200°C/400°F/Gas Mark 6. Heat 1 tablespoon of the oil in a large, non-stick frying pan, then add the mince and cook for 4–5 minutes, stirring occasionally until the meat changes colour. Remove from the pan.

2 Heat the remaining oil in the pan, then add the onion, garlic, celery and mushrooms and cook for 2–3 minutes, until soft.

3 Add the flour and cook over a medium heat, stirring constantly, for 1 minute. Gradually add the stock and bring to the boil, stirring constantly. Stir in the cream, Worcestershire sauce and peas, then add the mince, and season to taste with salt and pepper. Leave to bubble for 1–2 minutes.

4 Place the spaghetti in a shallow ovenproof dish, pour over the sauce and toss to combine well.

5 Scatter over the cheese and bake in the preheated oven for 15–20 minutes, until golden and piping hot. Serve immediately.

sicilian linguine

ingredients

serves 4

125 ml/4 fl oz olive oil,
    plus extra for brushing
2 aubergines, sliced
350 g/12 oz fresh beef mince
1 onion, chopped
2 garlic cloves, finely chopped
2 tbsp tomato purée
400 g/14 oz canned
    chopped tomatoes
1 tsp Worcestershire sauce
1 tbsp chopped fresh
    flat-leaf parsley
55 g/2 oz stoned black olives,
    sliced
1 red pepper, deseeded
    and chopped
175 g/6 oz dried linguine
115 g/4 oz freshly grated
    Parmesan cheese
salt and pepper

method

1 Preheat the oven to 200°C/400°F/Gas Mark 6. Brush a 20-cm/8-inch loose-based round cake tin with oil and line the base with baking paper. Heat half the oil in a frying pan. Add the aubergine in batches, and cook until lightly browned on both sides. Add more oil, as required. Drain the aubergine on kitchen paper, then arrange in overlapping slices to cover the base and sides of the cake tin, reserving a few slices.

2 Heat the remaining oil in a large saucepan and add the beef, onion and garlic. Cook over a medium heat, breaking up the meat with a wooden spoon, until browned all over. Add the tomato purée, tomatoes, Worcestershire sauce and parsley. Season to taste with salt and pepper and simmer for 10 minutes. Add the olives and red pepper and cook for a further 10 minutes.

3 Meanwhile, bring a saucepan of lightly salted water to the boil. Add the pasta, return to the boil and cook for 8–10 minutes, or until tender but still firm to the bite. Drain and transfer to a bowl. Add the meat sauce and Parmesan to the bowl and toss, then spoon into the cake tin, press down and cover with the remaining aubergine slices. Bake in the preheated oven for 40 minutes. Leave to stand for 5 minutes, then loosen around the edges and invert on to a plate. Remove and discard the baking paper and serve.

greek baked pasta

ingredients

serves 6

4 tbsp olive oil, plus extra
    for brushing
500 g/1 lb 2 oz
    fresh beef mince
1 small onion, finely chopped
2 garlic cloves, finely chopped
450 ml/16 fl oz passata
1 tsp sugar
2 tsp red wine vinegar
3 tbsp chopped fresh
    flat-leaf parsley
225 g/8 oz dried macaroni
225 g/8 oz Gruyère cheese,
    grated
1 kg/2 lb 4 oz aubergines,
    sliced lengthways
2 eggs, lightly beaten
100 g/3½ oz Parmesan
    cheese, grated
salt and pepper

white sauce

600 ml/1 pint milk
55 g/2 oz butter
55 g/2 oz plain flour

method

1 Heat half the oil in a saucepan and add the beef, onion and garlic. Cook over a medium heat, breaking up the meat with a wooden spoon, until browned all over. Stir in the passata, sugar, vinegar and parsley and season to taste with salt and pepper. Reduce the heat, cover and simmer for 15 minutes, until thickened.

2 Meanwhile, preheat the oven to 180°C/350°F/Gas Mark 4. Bring a large pan of salted water to the boil. Add the macaroni, return to the boil and cook for 8–10 minutes, until tender but still firm to the bite. Drain and return to the pan. Stir in the remaining oil and the Gruyère.

3 Preheat the grill to medium–high. Brush a large ovenproof dish with oil. Spread out the aubergine slices on a baking sheet and brush on both sides with oil. Cook under the preheated grill for 5 minutes on each side, until golden. Line the base and sides of the dish with the aubergine.

4 To make the white sauce, heat the milk, butter and flour in a saucepan, whisking constantly, until smooth and thick. Stir in the eggs and Parmesan. Spoon half the macaroni over the aubergine and pour in half the white sauce. Add the beef mixture and top with the remaining macaroni. Pour the remaining sauce over the top. Bake in the preheated oven for 35–40 minutes, until golden brown. Leave to stand for 10 minutes before serving.

pasta with aromatic beef sauce

ingredients

serves 4

2 tbsp sunflower oil
4 shallots, finely chopped
1 garlic clove, finely chopped
450 g/1 lb fresh beef mince
3 tbsp red wine
115 g/4 oz mushrooms,
    chopped
½ tsp ground cinnamon
½ tsp ground allspice
1 tbsp chopped fresh parsley
1 fresh basil sprig, leaves torn,
    plus extra sprigs to garnish
400 g/14 oz canned chopped
    tomatoes
2 tbsp tomato ketchup
350 g/12 oz dried conchiglie
    or other pasta shapes
salt and pepper

method

1 Heat the oil in a frying pan. Add the shallots and garlic and cook over a low heat, stirring occasionally, for 5 minutes, until softened. Add the beef, increase the heat to medium and cook, stirring frequently and breaking it up with a wooden spoon, for 8–10 minutes, until browned all over. Drain off as much fat as possible.

2 Stir in the wine and simmer over a low heat, stirring frequently, for 5 minutes. Add the mushrooms, cinnamon, allspice, parsley, torn basil, tomatoes and tomato ketchup, then season to taste with salt and pepper and mix well. Cover and simmer over a very low heat, stirring occasionally, for 1 hour. If the mixture seems to be drying out, add a little water.

3 Meanwhile, bring a large saucepan of salted water to the boil. Add the pasta, return to the boil and cook for 8–10 minutes, until tender but still firm to the bite. Drain and toss with the beef sauce. Garnish with basil sprigs and serve immediately.

one-pot pasta

ingredients

serves 4

2 tbsp olive oil
1 onion, chopped
1 garlic clove,
    finely chopped
1 celery stick, chopped
1 carrot, chopped
500 g/1 lb 2 oz
    fresh beef mince
115 g/4 oz mushrooms, sliced
400 g/14 oz canned
    chopped tomatoes
1 tbsp tomato purée
1 tsp sugar
pinch of dried oregano
1 tbsp chopped fresh
    flat-leaf parsley
175 g/6 oz dried fusilli
175 ml/6 fl oz red wine
1½ tbsp concentrated beef
    stock or 1 beef stock cube
salt and pepper

method

1 Heat the oil in a large saucepan with a tight-fitting lid. Add the onion, garlic, celery and carrot and cook over a low heat, stirring occasionally, for 5 minutes, until softened. Add the beef, increase the heat to medium and cook, stirring frequently and breaking up the meat with a wooden spoon, for 5–8 minutes, until evenly browned.

2 Add the mushrooms and cook for a further 3–4 minutes. Add the tomatoes, tomato purée, sugar, herbs, pasta and wine. Stir in the concentrated stock, add just enough water to cover and stir well.

3 Reduce the heat, cover tightly and simmer gently for 15–20 minutes, until the pasta is tender but still firm to the bite and the sauce has thickened. Season to taste with salt and pepper and serve immediately.

spaghetti bolognese

ingredients

serves 4

350 g/12 oz dried spaghetti
fresh Parmesan cheese shavings,
    to garnish (optional)
sprigs of thyme, to garnish
crusty bread, to serve

bolognese sauce

2 tbsp olive oil
1 onion, finely chopped
2 garlic cloves, finely chopped
1 carrot, finely chopped
85 g/3 oz mushrooms, sliced or
    chopped (optional)
1 tsp dried oregano
½ tsp dried thyme
1 bay leaf
280 g/10 oz fresh lean beef mince
300 ml/10 fl oz stock
300 ml/10 fl oz passata
salt and pepper

method

1 To make the sauce, heat the oil in a heavy-based, non-stick saucepan. Add the onion and cook, half covered, for 5 minutes, or until soft. Add the garlic, carrot and mushrooms, if using, and cook for a further 3 minutes, stirring occasionally.

2 Add the herbs and mince to the pan and cook until the meat has browned, stirring regularly.

3 Add the stock and passata. Reduce the heat, season to taste and cook over a medium–low heat, half covered, for 15–20 minutes, or until the sauce has reduced and thickened. Remove and discard the bay leaf.

4 Meanwhile, bring a large saucepan of lightly salted water to the boil. Add the pasta, bring back to the boil and cook for 8–10 minutes, until tender but still firm to the bite. Drain well and mix together the pasta and sauce until the pasta is well coated. Serve immediately with crusty bread and garnished with Parmesan cheese shavings, if using, and sprigs of thyme.

meatballs in tomato sauce

ingredients

serves 4

3 slices white bread,
   crusts removed
650 g/1 lb 7 oz fresh beef mince
1 onion, finely chopped
125 ml/4 fl oz tomato ketchup
1 egg, lightly beaten
3 tbsp water
salt and pepper
chopped fresh parsley,
   to garnish

tomato sauce

2 tbsp sunflower oil
1 onion, finely chopped
2 garlic cloves, finely chopped
2 tbsp tomato purée
100 ml/3½ fl oz water
400 g/14 oz canned chopped
   tomatoes
1–2 tsp brown sugar

method

1 Tear the bread into pieces, put it into a bowl and pour in enough water to cover. Leave to soak for 5 minutes.

2 Put the beef, onion, tomato ketchup and egg into a bowl and season to taste with salt and pepper. Squeeze out the bread, add it to the bowl and mix well with your hands until thoroughly combined and smooth. Add the 3 tablespoons of water and knead for 5 minutes. Set aside while you make the sauce.

3 For the tomato sauce, heat the oil in a saucepan. Add the onion and garlic and cook over a low heat, stirring occasionally, for 5 minutes, until softened. Meanwhile, mix the tomato purée with the 100 ml/3½ fl oz of water in a small bowl. Add to the saucepan with the tomatoes and bring to the boil, then simmer, stirring occasionally, for 15–20 minutes, until thickened. Transfer the sauce to a food processor or blender and process to a purée. Pour into a clean pan and stir in the sugar to taste.

4 Meanwhile, shape the beef mixture into 20 small meatballs, rolling them between the palms of your hands. Bring the sauce back to a simmer, then add the meatballs and simmer gently, occasionally shaking the pan, for 30 minutes, until cooked through. Transfer to a serving dish, garnish with parsley and serve immediately.

chicken meatball pasta

ingredients

serves 4

3 tbsp olive oil
1 red onion, chopped
400 g/14 oz fresh chicken mince
55 g/2 oz fresh white breadcrumbs
2 tsp dried oregano
1 garlic clove, crushed
400 g/14 oz canned chopped
    tomatoes
1 tbsp sun-dried tomato paste
300 ml/10 fl oz water
225 g/8 oz dried linguine
salt and pepper
Parmesan cheese shavings,
    to serve

method

1 Heat 1 tablespoon of the oil in a large frying pan and
    fry half the chopped onion for 5 minutes, until just
    softened. Leave to cool.

2 Place the chicken, breadcrumbs, oregano and the fried
    onion in a food processor or blender. Season well with
    salt and pepper, and process for 2–3 minutes, until
    thoroughly combined. Shape into 24 meatballs.

3 Heat the remaining oil in the frying pan and fry the
    meatballs over a medium–high heat for 3–4 minutes,
    until golden brown. Remove and set aside.

4 Add the remaining onion and the garlic to the pan and
    fry for 5 minutes. Stir in the tomatoes, sun-dried
    tomato paste and water, and bring to the boil. Add the
    meatballs and simmer for 20 minutes. Season to taste
    with salt and pepper.

5 Meanwhile, bring a large saucepan of lightly salted
    water to the boil. Add the pasta, bring back to the
    boil and cook for 8–10 minutes, until tender but still
    firm to the bite. Drain the pasta well and toss with the
    meatballs and sauce. Serve immediately with Parmesan
    cheese shavings.

penne with turkey meatballs

ingredients

serves 4

350 g/12 oz fresh turkey mince
1 small garlic clove, finely chopped
2 tbsp finely chopped fresh parsley
1 egg, lightly beaten
plain flour, for dusting
3 tbsp olive oil
1 onion, finely chopped
1 celery stick, finely chopped
1 carrot, finely chopped
400 ml/14 fl oz passata
1 fresh rosemary sprig
1 bay leaf
350 g/12 oz dried penne
salt and pepper
freshly grated Parmesan cheese,
    to serve

method

1 Put the turkey, garlic and parsley in a bowl and mix well. Stir in the egg and season to taste with salt and pepper. Dust your hands lightly with flour and shape the mixture into walnut-sized balls between your palms. Lightly dust each meatball with flour.

2 Heat the oil in a saucepan. Add the onion, celery and carrot and cook over a low heat, stirring occasionally, for 5 minutes, until softened. Increase the heat to medium, add the meatballs and cook, turning frequently, for 8–10 minutes, until golden brown all over.

3 Pour in the passata, add the rosemary and bay leaf, season to taste with salt and pepper and bring to the boil. Lower the heat, cover and simmer gently, stirring occasionally, for 40–45 minutes. Remove and discard the herbs.

4 Shortly before the meatballs are ready, bring a large pan of lightly salted water to the boil. Add the pasta, bring back to the boil and cook for 8–10 minutes, until tender but still firm to the bite. Drain and add to the pan with the meatballs. Stir gently and heat through briefly, then spoon into individual warmed dishes. Sprinkle with Parmesan cheese and serve immediately

one-pot chilli & rice

ingredients

serves 4

500 g/1 lb 2 oz fresh beef mince
1 large onion, finely chopped
2 garlic cloves, finely chopped
1 red pepper, deseeded and
    finely chopped
2 celery sticks, finely chopped
2 tsp hot chilli powder
1 tsp cumin seeds
2 tbsp tomato purée
225 g/8 oz brown basmati rice
400 g/14 oz canned chopped
    tomatoes
2 tsp cocoa powder
600 ml/1 pint beef stock
400 g/14 oz canned black beans,
    drained and rinsed
salt and pepper
sour cream and nachos, to serve

method

1 Dry-fry the mince in a large, deep flameproof casserole
   or saucepan for 4–5 minutes, until starting to brown.
   Add the onion, garlic, red pepper and celery and
   continue cooking for a further 2–3 minutes, stirring
   constantly. Add the chilli powder and cumin seeds and
   cook for 1–2 minutes.

2 Add the tomato purée and cook for a further 1 minute,
   stirring constantly. Stir in the rice, tomatoes, cocoa
   powder and stock, season to taste with salt and pepper,
   then cover and cook for 20 minutes, stirring occasionally.

3 Stir in the beans and continue to cook for a further
   10 minutes, until the rice is fully cooked. Serve with
   sour cream to drizzle over and nachos on the side.

chinese noodles with beef & shredded vegetables

ingredients

serves 4

500 g/1 lb 2 oz dried egg
    noodles
3 tbsp groundnut oil
3 spring onions, thinly sliced
2 garlic cloves, finely chopped
1-cm/$\frac{1}{2}$-inch piece fresh
    ginger, finely chopped
350 g/12 oz fresh beef mince
1 tbsp sesame oil
5 tbsp soy sauce
2 tbsp Chinese rice wine or
    dry sherry
1 tbsp sugar
1 tbsp cornflour
4 tbsp water

to serve

115 g/4 oz fresh beansprouts,
    blanched
115g/4 oz Chinese leaves,
    blanched and shredded
115 g/4 oz carrots, blanched
    and shredded
115 g/4 oz cucumber, shredded
115 g/4 oz radishes, shredded

method

1 Put the beansprouts and shredded vegetables into
    small serving dishes and set aside. Cook the noodles in
    a large pan of salted boiling water according to the
    packet instructions, then drain and keep warm.

2 Meanwhile, heat a wok over a medium heat, then add
    the groundnut oil and swirl it around the pan to heat.
    Add the spring onions, garlic and ginger and stir-fry for
    2 minutes. Add the beef and stir-fry, breaking it up with
    a wooden spoon, for 5 minutes, until evenly browned.
    Stir in the sesame oil, soy sauce, rice wine and sugar
    and cook, stirring constantly, for a further 3 minutes.

3 Mix the cornflour to a paste with the water in a small
    bowl and add to the wok. Simmer, stirring constantly,
    until the sauce has thickened and become glossy.

4 Divide the noodles between individual warmed
    bowls and top with the beef mixture and shredded
    vegetables. Serve immediately.

chinese-style fried rice

ingredients

serves 4

2 tbsp vegetable oil

4 eggs, beaten

250 g/9 oz fresh chicken mince

1 bunch spring onions,
    trimmed and finely chopped

2 garlic cloves, finely chopped

2 tsp Chinese five-spice powder

400 g/14 oz basmati rice,
    cooked, cooled and chilled

100 g/3½ oz cooked prawns

125 g/4½ oz frozen peas

100 g/3½ oz canned sweetcorn,
    drained

25 g/1 oz fresh coriander,
    finely chopped

1 tsp toasted sesame oil

salt and pepper

method

1 Heat 1 tablespoon of the vegetable oil in a wok or large,
non-stick frying pan. Season the eggs to taste with salt
and pepper, then add to the wok and gently whisk with
a fork until lightly cooked. Remove from the wok and
roughly chop. Wipe out the wok with kitchen paper.

2 Heat the remaining oil in the wok, add the mince and fry
for 4–5 minutes, until it changes colour and crumbles.

3 Add the spring onions, garlic and five-spice powder
and cook for a further 1–2 minutes, stirring constantly.

4 Add the rice, prawns, peas, sweetcorn and half the
coriander. Stir-fry until everything is piping hot.

5 Stir in the cooked egg, sesame oil, and salt and pepper
to taste, scatter over the remaining coriander and
serve immediately.

variation

Use 250 g/9 oz fresh pork mince instead of chicken,
55 g/2 oz shiitake mushrooms instead of the sweetcorn
and omit the cooked prawns.

burgers & kebabs

classic cheeseburgers

ingredients

serves 4

750 g/1 lb 10 oz fresh beef mince
1 beef stock cube
1 tbsp minced dried onion
2 tbsp water
1–2 tbsp sunflower oil
55 g/2 oz Cheddar cheese,
  grated

to serve

lettuce leaves
4 burger buns, split
tomato slices
chips

method

1 Place the beef in a large mixing bowl. Crumble the stock cube over the meat, add the dried onion and water and mix well. Divide the meat into 4 portions, shape each into a ball, then flatten slightly to make a patty of your preferred thickness.

2 Place a griddle pan over a medium–high heat. Lightly brush the burgers with oil and cook for 5–6 minutes. Turn the burgers, sprinkle the cheese over the cooked side and cook for a further 5–6 minutes, or until cooked to your liking.

3 Place the lettuce leaves on the bottom halves of the buns and top with the burgers. Place a couple of tomato slices on top and add the lids. Serve immediately with chips.

cheese-stuffed burgers

ingredients

serves 4

500 g/1 lb 2 oz fresh beef
    mince
1 onion, finely chopped
1 garlic clove, finely chopped
1 tsp creamed horseradish
1 tbsp chopped fresh thyme
55 g/2 oz Gorgonzola,
    Lancashire or feta cheese,
    crumbled
4 burger buns, split and toasted
salt and pepper
rocket leaves, to serve

method

1 Preheat the grill to medium–high. Put the beef, onion, garlic, horseradish and thyme into a bowl. Season to taste with salt and pepper and mix well until thoroughly combined. Divide the mixture into 8 portions and shape each portion into a patty shape.

2 Sprinkle the cheese over 4 of the patties and top with the remaining patties. Gently press the edges together, smoothing them with a palette knife to enclose the cheese completely.

3 Cook under the preheated grill for 5–6 minutes on each side, turning them carefully with a fish slice. Serve in the toasted buns with rocket leaves.

cheese & apple burgers

ingredients

serves 4

450 g/1 lb fresh best steak mince
1 onion, finely chopped
1–2 tsp wholegrain mustard,
    or to taste
2–3 tsp Worcestershire sauce
55 g/2 oz mature Cheddar cheese,
    grated
2 Bramley apples
1 tsp butter, melted
2–3 tsp caster sugar
55 g/2 oz Gruyère cheese,
    thinly sliced
4 burger buns, split and toasted
salt and pepper
spinach leaves, to serve

method

1 Place the steak mince in a large bowl. Add the onion, mustard, salt and pepper, Worcestershire sauce to taste and the grated cheese. Peel and core 1 of the apples, then grate and add to the bowl. Mix together, then shape into 4 equal-sized burgers. Cover and leave to chill for 30 minutes.

2 Preheat the grill to medium–high. Peel and core the remaining apple, then cut into 4–6 thick slices. Brush with the melted butter and sprinkle with the caster sugar. Place on a foil-lined grill rack and cook under the hot grill for 2–3 minutes on each side, or until caramelized. Reserve.

3 Cook the burgers under the hot grill for 4–6 minutes on each side, or until cooked to personal preference. Top the burgers with the sliced cheese and grill until the cheese has melted. Serve in the toasted buns with fresh spinach leaves and the caramelized apple slices.

variation

Use 450 g/1 lb lean pork mince instead of steak.

blt burgers with asparagus

ingredients

serves 4–6

225 g/8 oz back bacon rashers
450 g/1 lb fresh steak mince
1 onion, grated
2–4 garlic cloves, crushed
salt and pepper

dip

175 g/6 oz baby asparagus spears
1 tbsp lemon juice
1 small ripe avocado, peeled,
    stoned and finely chopped
2 firm tomatoes, peeled, deseeded
    and finely chopped
150 ml/5 fl oz crème fraîche
salt and pepper

to serve

lettuce leaves
burger buns, split
tomato slices

method

1 Remove any rind and fat from the bacon rashers and chop finely. Place the bacon, steak mince, onion, garlic and salt and pepper in a large bowl and mix well. Shape into 4–6 equal-sized burgers, then cover and leave to chill in the refrigerator for 30 minutes.

2 To make the dip, trim the asparagus and cook in a saucepan of lightly salted boiling water for 5 minutes, then drain and plunge into cold water. When cold, drain and finely chop half the spears into a bowl and reserve the rest to serve. Sprinkle the lemon juice over the avocado. Stir the avocado, tomatoes and crème fraîche into the chopped asparagus. Add salt and pepper to taste, cover and leave to chill until required.

3 Preheat the grill to medium–high. Place the burgers on a foil-lined grill rack and cook under the hot grill for 3–5 minutes on each side, or until they are cooked to personal preference.

4 Place the lettuce leaves on the bottom halves of the burger buns and top with the burgers. Top with a tomato slice, an asparagus spear and a spoonful of the dip. Add the lids and serve immediately.

italian steak melt burgers

ingredients

serves 4

450 g/1 lb fresh best steak mince
1 onion, grated
2–4 garlic cloves, crushed
1 small red pepper, deseeded,
    peeled and chopped
55 g/2 oz stoned black olives,
    finely chopped
pepper
1 tbsp tomato purée
2 large tomatoes, thickly sliced
85 g/3 oz Gruyère cheese, sliced
4 burger buns, split and toasted
salad leaves, to serve

method

1 Place the steak mince, onion, garlic, red pepper, olives, pepper and tomato purée in a food processor or blender and, using the pulse button, blend together. Shape into 4 equal-sized burgers, then cover and leave to chill for at least 30 minutes.

2 Preheat the grill to medium–high. Place the burgers on a foil-lined grill rack and cook under the preheated grill for 3–5 minutes on each side, or until they are cooked to personal preference.

3 Place a tomato slice on top of each burger, then place the cheese over the tomato. Grill for a further 2–3 minutes, or until the cheese begins to melt. Serve in the toasted buns with salad leaves.

beef & beetroot burgers

ingredients

serves 4

3 tbsp sunflower oil
1 onion, finely chopped
650 g/1 lb 7 oz fresh beef mince
1 small egg, lightly beaten
2 tsp white wine vinegar
½ tsp paprika
1 tbsp finely chopped drained
    capers
3 tbsp finely chopped cooked
    beetroot
2 tbsp soured cream
55 g/2 oz butter
4 eggs
salt and pepper

method

1 Heat 1 tablespoon of the oil in a frying pan. Add the onion and cook over a low heat, stirring occasionally, for 5 minutes, until softened.

2 Transfer the onion to a large bowl and add the beef, egg, vinegar, paprika and capers and mix well with your hands. Add the beetroot and soured cream, season to taste with salt and pepper and mix well again. Shape the mixture into 4 patties.

3 Melt 25 g/1 oz of the butter with the remaining oil in a frying pan. Add the burgers and cook over a medium heat for 6–7 minutes on each side, until well browned. Remove with a fish slice and drain on kitchen paper.

4 Melt half the remaining butter in a frying pan. Break two of the eggs into separate cups and slide them into the pan. Immediately collect the whites around the yolks with a slotted spoon to keep them neat and separated and cook for a few minutes until the whites have set but the yolks are still runny; keep warm. Cook the remaining eggs in the remaining butter in the same way. Transfer the burgers to a warmed serving dish, top with the fried eggs and serve immediately.

beef & bacon burgers

ingredients

serves 6

650 g/1 lb 7 oz fresh beef
    mince
1 large onion, very finely
    chopped
1 garlic clove, very finely
    chopped (optional)
85 g/3 oz fresh breadcrumbs
2 tsp chopped fresh sage
1 large egg, lightly beaten
6 bacon rashers
40 g/1½ oz butter, melted
salt and pepper

method

1 Preheat the grill to medium–high. Put the beef, onion,
   garlic (if using), breadcrumbs, sage and egg into a
   bowl, season to taste with salt and pepper and mix
   well until thoroughly combined. Divide the mixture
   into 6 equal portions and shape into balls, then gently
   flatten into patties.

2 Wrap a bacon rasher around each patty and secure
   with a wooden cocktail stick.

3 Brush one side of each burger with a little of the
   melted butter and cook under the preheated grill for
   5 minutes. Carefully turn the burgers with a fish slice,
   brush with the remaining melted butter and grill for a
   further 4–5 minutes, until cooked to your liking.

4 Remove and discard the cocktail sticks. Serve
   immediately.

chilli burgers with coriander & spring onions

ingredients

serves 4

200 g/7 oz canned red kidney
 beans, drained and rinsed
450 g/1 lb fresh best steak mince
1–2 fresh red chillies, deseeded
 and chopped, or to taste
2–4 garlic cloves, crushed
6 spring onions, chopped
1 tbsp chopped fresh coriander
4 taco shells
shredded lettuce
grated carrot
soured cream
salt and pepper

salsa

3 ripe tomatoes, peeled and
 finely chopped
1 small ripe avocado, peeled,
 stoned and mashed
4 spring onions, finely chopped
1 fresh red chilli, deseeded and
 finely chopped
1 tbsp chopped fresh coriander

method

1 Place the kidney beans in a food processor and blend for 1 minute.

2 Add the steak mince, chillies, garlic, spring onions, coriander and salt and pepper to the food processor and blend for a further 2 minutes. Shape into 4 equal-sized burgers, then cover and leave to chill for 30 minutes.

3 Meanwhile, make the salsa. Mix the tomatoes, avocado, spring onions, chilli and coriander together. Place in a small bowl, cover and leave for at least 30 minutes to allow the flavours to develop.

4 Heat a non-stick frying pan until hot. When hot, add the burgers and cook over a medium heat for 3–5 minutes on each side, until golden or until cooked to personal preference.

5 Heat the taco shells according to the packet instructions and fill with shredded lettuce and grated carrot. Serve alongside the burgers, topped with the salsa and soured cream to serve.

sloppy joes

ingredients

serves 4–6

675 g/1 lb 8 oz fresh lean
   beef mince
½ onion, diced
2 garlic cloves, finely chopped
1 green pepper, deseeded
   and diced
450 ml/16 fl oz water
175 ml/6 fl oz tomato ketchup
1½ tbsp soft light brown sugar
dash of Worcestershire sauce
1 tsp Dijon mustard
1½ tsp salt
½ tsp black pepper
cayenne pepper, to taste
burger buns, split

method

1 Put the beef and onion into a large cold frying pan and place over a medium heat. Cook, stirring, breaking up the meat into very small pieces with a wooden spoon, until it begins to brown.

2 Add the garlic and green pepper and cook, stirring, for 2 minutes. Add half the water. Cook until simmering, scraping up any sediment from the base of the pan.

3 Stir in the tomato ketchup, sugar, Worcestershire sauce, mustard, salt, black pepper, cayenne pepper and the remaining water. Bring to simmering point, reduce the heat to low, and simmer for 30–45 minutes, or until most of the liquid has evaporated and the meat mixture is thick, rich and tender. Spoon the beef mixture onto each bun base. Add the bun lids and serve immediately.

bacon-wrapped chicken burgers

ingredients

serves 4

450 g/1 lb fresh chicken mince
1 onion, finely chopped
2 garlic cloves, crushed
55 g/2 oz pine kernels, toasted
55 g/2 oz Gruyère cheese, grated
2 tbsp fresh snipped chives
2 tbsp wholemeal flour
8 slices lean back bacon
1–2 tbsp sunflower oil
salt and pepper

to serve

crusty rolls, split
red onion slices
lettuce leaves
mayonnaise
spring onions, chopped

method

1 Place the chicken mince, onion, garlic, pine kernels, Gruyère cheese, chives and salt and pepper in a food processor or blender. Using the pulse button, blend the mixture together using short sharp bursts. Scrape out onto a board and shape into 4 even-sized burgers. Coat in the flour, then cover and chill for 1 hour.

2 Wrap each burger with 2 bacon slices, securing in place with a wooden cocktail stick.

3 Heat a heavy-based frying pan and add the oil. When hot, add the burgers and cook over a medium heat for 5–6 minutes on each side, or until cooked through.

4 Remove and discard the cocktail sticks. Serve the burgers in the crusty rolls with the red onion, lettuce, a spoonful of mayonnaise and spring onions. Serve immediately.

turkey & tarragon burgers

ingredients

serves 4

55 g/2 oz bulgar wheat
450 g/1 lb fresh turkey mince
1 tbsp finely grated orange rind
1 red onion, finely chopped
1 yellow pepper, deseeded,
    peeled and finely chopped
25 g/1 oz toasted flaked almonds
1 tbsp chopped fresh tarragon
salt and pepper

to serve

lettuce leaves
tomato and onion salad

method

1 Cook the bulgar wheat in a saucepan of lightly salted boiling water for 10–15 minutes, or according to the packet instructions.

2 Drain the bulgar wheat and place in a bowl with the turkey mince, orange rind, onion, yellow pepper, almonds, tarragon and salt and pepper to taste. Mix together, then shape into 4 equal-sized burgers. Cover and leave to chill in the refrigerator for 1 hour.

3 Preheat the grill to medium–high. Place the burgers on a foil-lined grill rack and cook under the hot grill for 3–5 minutes on each side, or until cooked through.

4 Put a few lettuce leaves on serving plates and place a burger on top of each. Serve immediately with a tomato and onion salad.

turkey & bean burgers

ingredients

serves 6

200 g/7 oz canned red kidney
    beans, drained and rinsed
½ bunch spring onions, trimmed
    and finely chopped
1 garlic clove, crushed
500 g/1 lb 2 oz fresh turkey mince
4 tbsp sweet chilli sauce
pinch of dried chilli flakes
vegetable oil, for frying
salt and pepper

to serve

toasted ciabatta rolls
fresh rocket leaves
tomato slices

method

1 Place the beans in a mixing bowl and crush with the
back of a fork. Add the spring onions, garlic, mince,
chilli sauce, chilli flakes and salt and pepper to taste.
Use your fingertips to combine.

2 Shape the mixture into 6 burger shapes. Heat the oil in
a frying pan, add the burgers and cook for 6–7 minutes
on each side, until thoroughly cooked.

3 Serve immediately in toasted ciabatta rolls with rocket
leaves and sliced tomatoes.

maple-glazed turkey burgers

ingredients

serves 4

2 fresh corn cobs (in their husks)
450 g/1 lb fresh turkey mince
1 red pepper, deseeded
    and finely chopped
6 spring onions, finely chopped
55 g/2 oz fresh white breadcrumbs
2 tbsp chopped fresh basil
2 tbsp maple syrup
salt and pepper

to serve

rocket leaves
tomato slices
cheese-topped burger buns, split
sweetcorn relish

method

1 Heat a griddle pan until hot, then add the sweetcorn cobs and cook over a medium–high heat, turning occasionally, for 8–10 minutes, or until the husks are charred. Remove from the griddle pan and leave to cool, then strip off the husks and silks. Using a sharp knife, cut away the kernels and place in a bowl.

2 Add the turkey mince, red pepper, spring onions, breadcrumbs and basil to the sweetcorn kernels in the bowl. Season to taste with salt and pepper. Mix together, then shape into 4 equal-sized burgers. Cover and leave to chill in the refrigerator for 1 hour.

3 Preheat the grill to medium–high. Place the burgers on a foil-lined grill rack, brush with maple syrup and cook under the hot grill for 3–5 minutes on each side, or until cooked through.

4 Place the rocket and tomato slices on the bottom halves of the buns and top with the burgers. Spoon over a little relish, add the lids and serve immediately.

mexican turkey burgers

ingredients

serves 4

450 g/1 lb fresh turkey mince
200 g/7 oz canned refried beans
2–4 garlic cloves, crushed
1–2 fresh jalapeño chillies,
    deseeded and finely chopped
2 tbsp tomato purée
1 tbsp chopped fresh coriander
salt and pepper

to serve

shredded baby spinach leaves
4 cheese-topped burger buns, split
salsa
guacamole
tortilla chips

method

1 Place the turkey mince in a bowl and break up any large lumps. Beat the refried beans until smooth, then add to the turkey in the bowl.

2 Add the garlic, chillies, tomato purée and coriander with salt and pepper to taste and mix together. Shape into 4 equal-sized burgers, then cover and leave to chill in the refrigerator for 1 hour.

3 Preheat the grill to medium–high. Place the burgers on a foil-lined grill rack and cook under the hot grill for 3–5 minutes on each side, or until cooked through.

4 Place the spinach on the bottom halves of the burger buns and top with the burgers. Spoon over a little salsa and guacamole and top with the lids. Serve immediately with tortilla chips on the side.

lemon & herb burgers

ingredients

serves 4

250 g/9 oz fresh chicken mince
1 garlic clove, crushed
1 tbsp clear honey
finely grated zest of 1 lemon
juice of ½ lemon
1 tbsp fresh thyme leaves,
    finely chopped
½ bunch spring onions,
    trimmed and finely chopped
1–2 tbsp vegetable oil,
    for frying
salt and pepper

method

1 Put the mince, garlic, honey, lemon zest, lemon juice, thyme, spring onions and salt and pepper to taste into a bowl and use your fingertips to combine. Shape the mixture into 4 burgers, transfer to a plate, cover and leave to chill in the refrigerator for at least 30 minutes.

2 Heat the oil in a frying pan over a medium heat, then add the burgers and cook for 5–7 minutes on each side, until the chicken is thoroughly cooked. Serve the burgers immediately.

yakitori-style chicken burgers

ingredients

serves 4

250 g/9 oz fresh chicken mince
1 tbsp grated fresh ginger
1 garlic clove, finely chopped
1 tbsp ketjap manis or 2 tsp soy
    sauce and 1 tsp honey
½ bunch spring onions,
    trimmed and finely chopped
1–2 tbsp vegetable oil
fresh mango salsa and noodle
    salad, to serve

method

1 Put the mince, ginger, garlic, ketjap manis and spring onions into a bowl and use your fingertips to combine. Shape the mixture into 4 burgers, transfer to a plate, cover and leave to chill for at least 30 minutes.

2 Preheat a griddle pan over a medium heat, then add the oil. Add the burgers and cook for 5–6 minutes on each side, until the chicken is thoroughly cooked. Serve immediately with mango salsa and noodle salad.

beef keftas

ingredients

serves 6–8

1 kg/2 lb 4 oz fresh beef
    mince
1 Spanish onion, grated
3 garlic cloves, very finely
    chopped
4 tbsp chopped fresh coriander
1 tsp ground cumin
½ tsp ground cinnamon
½ tsp ground turmeric
1 tsp paprika
1 large egg, lightly beaten
3 tbsp finely chopped fresh mint,
    plus extra leaves to garnish
150 ml/5 fl oz natural yogurt
sunflower oil, for brushing
salt and pepper
lime wedges, to garnish

method

1 Put the beef, onion, garlic, coriander and spices into a bowl and season to taste with salt and pepper. Add the egg and mix well with your hands until thoroughly combined and very smooth. Cover the bowl with clingfilm and chill in the refrigerator for 30 minutes.

2 Meanwhile, mix the chopped mint and the yogurt together in a bowl and season to taste with salt. Cover with clingfilm and chill until required.

3 Preheat the grill to medium–high. Remove the beef mixture from the refrigerator, scoop up pieces with your hands and shape into small ovals about 2 cm/³/₄ inch thick. Thread the keftas onto metal or pre-soaked wooden skewers, with three to each skewer.

4 Brush the grill rack with oil. Cook the skewers, in batches if necessary, under the preheated grill, turning occasionally, for 10–12 minutes, until cooked through. Garnish with mint leaves and lime wedges and serve immediately with the minted yogurt.

indian kebabs

ingredients

serves 4

1 onion, finely chopped

2 garlic cloves, finely chopped

4-cm/1½-inch piece fresh
   ginger, finely chopped

2 fresh green chillies, deseeded
   and finely chopped

½ tsp ground turmeric

2 tbsp chopped fresh coriander,
   plus extra to garnish

3 tbsp natural yogurt, plus extra
   to serve

1 tbsp lemon juice

650 g/1 lb 7 oz fresh beef mince

4 tbsp fresh breadcrumbs

melted butter, for brushing

salt

tomato and onion salad and
   warm naan bread, to serve

method

1 Put the onion, garlic, ginger, chillies, turmeric, coriander,
   yogurt, lemon juice, beef and breadcrumbs into a bowl.
   Season to taste with salt and mix well with your hands
   until thoroughly combined. Cover with clingfilm and
   leave to rest at room temperature for 30 minutes.

2 Preheat the grill to medium–high. Brush 12 metal or
   pre-soaked wooden skewers with melted butter.
   Dampen your hands and shape the beef mixture into
   24 oval shapes. Thread 2 onto each prepared skewer
   and place them in the grill pan.

3 Brush with a little melted butter and cook under
   the preheated grill, in batches if necessary, for
   5 minutes. Turn the skewers, brush with more melted
   butter and cook for a further 4 minutes, until the
   kebabs are cooked through and browned.

4 Transfer the kebabs to a warmed serving dish, drizzle
   with yogurt and garnish with coriander. Serve
   immediately with tomato and onion salad and
   naan bread.

bakes &
casseroles

lasagne al forno

ingredients

serves 6

55 g/2 oz butter
100 g/3½ oz pancetta
1 onion, finely chopped
1 celery stick, finely chopped
1 carrot, finely chopped
350 g/12 oz fresh beef mince
5 tbsp red wine
2 tbsp sun-dried tomato purée
2 eggs
150 g/5½ oz freshly grated
    Parmesan cheese
30 g/1 oz fresh breadcrumbs
2 tbsp olive oil
350 g/12 oz ricotta cheese
8 dried no pre-cook lasagne sheets
350 g/12 oz mozzarella cheese,
    sliced
salt and pepper
chopped fresh parsley, to garnish

method

1 Heat the butter in a large saucepan. Add the pancetta, onion, celery and carrot and cook over a low heat, until soft. Increase the heat to medium, add half the mince and cook until evenly browned. Stir in the wine and tomato purée, season with salt and pepper and bring to the boil. Reduce the heat, cover and simmer gently for 1½ hours, until the steak is tender.

2 Mix the rest of the mince in a bowl with 1 egg, 1 tablespoon of the Parmesan cheese and the breadcrumbs. Shape into walnut-sized balls.

3 Heat the oil in a frying pan, add the meatballs and cook for 5–8 minutes, until brown. Pass the ricotta through a sieve into a bowl. Stir in the remaining egg and 4 tablespoons of the remaining Parmesan cheese.

4 Preheat the oven to 180°C/350°F/Gas Mark 4. In a rectangular ovenproof dish, make layers with the lasagne sheets, ricotta mixture, meat sauce, meatballs, and mozzarella cheese. Finish with a layer of the ricotta mixture and sprinkle with the remaining Parmesan cheese. Bake the lasagne in the preheated oven for 20–25 minutes, until golden and bubbling. Serve immediately, garnished with chopped parsley.

beef en croûte

ingredients

serves 4

butter, for greasing
350 g/12 oz fresh beef mince
2 onions, finely chopped
1 garlic clove, finely chopped
55 g/2 oz fresh breadcrumbs
2 Bramley apples, peeled,
    cored and finely chopped
1 tbsp Dijon mustard
2 tbsp chopped fresh parsley
2 eggs
4 tbsp beef stock
300 g/10½ oz ready-made puff
    pastry, thawed if frozen
plain flour, for dusting
salt and pepper

method

1 Preheat the oven to 180°C/350°F/Gas Mark 4. Grease a 650-g/1 lb 7-oz loaf tin with butter. Put the beef, onions, garlic, breadcrumbs, apples, mustard and parsley into a bowl and mix well. Beat one of the eggs with the stock and add to the bowl. Season to taste with salt and pepper and mix until combined.

2 Spoon the mixture into the prepared tin. Bake in the preheated oven for 45 minutes. Remove from the oven, and pour off any fat. Leave to cool completely and turn out when cold.

3 Preheat the oven to 220°C/425°F/Gas Mark 7. Roll out the pastry on a lightly floured surface to a thickness of 3–5 mm/⅛–¼ inch. Put the meatloaf in the centre, brush the edges of the pastry with water and fold over to enclose the meat completely, trimming off any excess pastry. Put the parcel, seam-side down, on a baking sheet. Roll out the trimmings and use to make decorations. Brush with water and arrange on top of the parcel. Lightly beat the remaining egg and brush it over the parcel, then make 2–3 slits in the pastry.

4 Bake in the preheated oven for 35 minutes, until puffed up and golden brown. Reduce the oven temperature to 180°C/350°F/Gas Mark 4 and bake for a further 10 minutes. Serve immediately.

meatloaf

ingredients

serves 4

500 g/1 lb 2 oz fresh beef mince
1 onion, finely chopped
2 garlic cloves, finely chopped
    (optional)
115 g/4 oz mushrooms,
    finely chopped
85 g/3 oz fresh breadcrumbs
2 eggs, lightly beaten
2 tsp Dijon mustard
1 tsp Worcestershire sauce
1 tsp celery salt
1 tbsp chopped fresh parsley
8–10 streaky bacon rashers
pepper

tomato sauce

2 tbsp sunflower oil
1 onion, finely chopped
2 garlic cloves, finely chopped
2 tbsp tomato purée
100 ml/3½ fl oz water
400 g/14 oz canned chopped
    tomatoes

method

1 Preheat the oven to 160°C/325°F/Gas Mark 3. Put the beef, onion, garlic (if using), mushrooms, breadcrumbs, eggs, mustard, Worcestershire sauce, celery salt and parsley into a bowl. Season to taste with pepper and mix well until thoroughly combined.

2 Spoon the mixture into a 900-g/2-lb loaf tin, pressing it down well. Cover with the bacon. Put the loaf tin into a roasting tin and pour in boiling water to come about halfway up the sides. Bake in the preheated oven for 1½ hours, until a wooden cocktail stick inserted into the centre comes out clean.

3 Meanwhile, make the tomato sauce. Heat the oil in a saucepan, add the onion and garlic and cook over a low heat, stirring occasionally, for 5 minutes, until softened. Add the tomato purée, water, tomatoes and bring to the boil then simmer for 15–20 minutes.

4 Remove the tin from the oven and leave to cool for 10 minutes. Drain off any excess liquid and turn out onto a board. Cut into slices and serve with the tomato sauce.

american-style lasagne

ingredients

serves 4

2 tbsp olive oil
55 g/2 oz pancetta or bacon, chopped
1 garlic clove, finely chopped
1 onion, chopped
225 g/8 oz fresh beef mince
2 carrots, chopped
2 celery sticks, chopped
115 g/4 oz mushrooms, chopped
pinch of dried oregano
5 tbsp red wine
150 ml/5 fl oz beef stock
1 tbsp sun-dried tomato paste
225 g/8 oz dried no pre-cook lasagne sheets
115 g/4 oz Parmesan cheese, grated
400 g/14 oz canned chopped tomatoes
few fresh basil leaves, torn
salt and pepper
mixed salad, to serve

method

1 Heat the oil in a large saucepan. Add the pancetta and cook over a medium heat, stirring occasionally, for 2–3 minutes. Reduce the heat to low, add the garlic and onion and cook, stirring occasionally, for 5 minutes, until softened.

2 Add the beef, increase the heat to medium and cook, stirring frequently and breaking it up with a wooden spoon, for 8–10 minutes, until evenly browned. Stir in the carrots, celery and mushrooms and cook, stirring occasionally, for a further 5 minutes. Add the oregano, pour in the wine and stock and stir in the sun-dried tomato paste. Season to taste with salt and pepper. Bring to the boil, reduce the heat and simmer for 40 minutes.

3 Preheat the oven to 190°C/375°F/Gas Mark 5. Make alternating layers of the beef sauce, lasagne sheets and Parmesan in a large, rectangular ovenproof dish. Pour the tomatoes over the top to cover completely. Bake in the preheated oven for 30 minutes. Remove the dish from the oven and leave to stand for 10 minutes, then sprinkle with torn basil, cut into four and serve with a mixed salad.

chicken lasagne

ingredients

serves 6

2 tbsp olive oil
900 g/2 lb fresh chicken mince
1 garlic clove, finely chopped
4 carrots, chopped
4 leeks, sliced
450 ml/16 fl oz chicken stock
2 tbsp tomato purée
115 g/4 oz Cheddar cheese, grated
1 tsp Dijon mustard
115 g/4 oz dried no pre-cook
   lasagne sheets
salt and pepper

white sauce

600 ml/1 pint milk
55 g/2 oz butter
55 g/2 oz plain flour

method

1 Preheat the oven to 190°C/375°F/Gas Mark 5. Heat the oil in a heavy-based saucepan. Add the chicken and cook over a medium heat, breaking it up with a wooden spoon, for 5 minutes, or until it is browned all over. Add the garlic, carrots and leeks and cook, stirring occasionally, for 5 minutes.

2 Stir in the stock and tomato purée and season to taste with salt and pepper. Bring to the boil, reduce the heat, cover and simmer for 30 minutes.

3 Meanwhile, make the white sauce. Heat the milk, butter and flour in a saucepan, whisking constantly, until smooth and thick. Season to taste with salt and pepper, and stir in half the cheese and the mustard.

4 In a large ovenproof dish, make alternate layers of the chicken mixture, lasagne sheets and cheese sauce, ending with a layer of cheese sauce. Sprinkle with the remaining cheese and bake in the preheated oven for 1 hour, or until golden brown and bubbling. Serve the lasagne immediately.

chicken & mushroom lasagne

ingredients

serves 4–6

2 tbsp olive oil
1 large onion, finely chopped
500 g/1 lb 2 oz fresh chicken or
    turkey mince
100 g/3½ oz smoked pancetta,
    chopped
250 g/9 oz chestnut mushrooms,
    chopped
100 g/3½ oz dried ceps, soaked
150 ml/5 fl oz dry white wine
400 g/14 oz canned chopped
    tomatoes
3 tbsp chopped fresh basil leaves
9 dried no pre-cook lasagne sheets
3 tbsp finely grated Parmesan
    cheese
salt and pepper

white sauce

600 ml/1 pint milk
55 g/2 oz butter
55 g/2 oz plain flour

method

1 Preheat the oven to 190°C/375°F/Gas Mark 5. For the white sauce, heat the milk, butter and flour in a saucepan, whisking constantly, until smooth and thick. Season to taste with salt and pepper, cover and leave to stand.

2 Heat the oil in a large saucepan and fry the onion, stirring, for 3–4 minutes. Add the chicken and pancetta and cook for 6–8 minutes. Stir in both types of mushrooms and cook for a further 2–3 minutes.

3 Add the wine and bring to the boil. Pour in the tomatoes and their can juices, cover and simmer for 20 minutes. Stir in the basil.

4 Arrange 3 of the lasagne sheets in a rectangular ovenproof dish, then spoon over a third of the meat sauce. Spread a third of the white sauce over the meat. Repeat the layers twice more, finishing with a layer of white sauce.

5 Sprinkle with the cheese and bake in the preheated oven for 35–40 minutes, until the topping is golden and bubbling. Serve immediately.

turkey pasta bake

ingredients

serves 4–6

100 g/3½ oz butter
1 tbsp olive oil
1 onion, finely chopped
450 g/1 lb fresh turkey mince
2 tbsp plain flour
700 ml/1¼ pints milk
1 tsp Dijon mustard
85 g/3 oz Cheddar cheese,
    grated
280 g/10 oz dried macaroni
2 tbsp chopped fresh parsley
85 g/3 oz fresh breadcrumbs

method

1 Melt 25 g/1 oz of the butter with the oil in a frying pan. Add the onion and cook over a low heat, stirring occasionally, for 5 minutes until soft. Add the turkey, increase the heat to medium and cook, stirring frequently, for 7–8 minutes, until evenly browned. Remove the pan from the heat, transfer the turkey and onion to a bowl with a slotted spoon and set aside.

2 Melt 40 g/1½ oz of the remaining butter in a saucepan, stir in the flour and cook, stirring constantly, for 1 minute. Remove the pan from the heat and gradually whisk in the milk, then return to the heat and bring to the boil, whisking constantly until thickened. Remove the pan from the heat and stir in the mustard, turkey mixture and 55 g/2 oz of the cheese.

3 Preheat the oven to 180°C/350°F/Gas Mark 4. Bring a large saucepan of lightly salted water to the boil. Add the pasta, bring back to the boil and cook for 8–10 minutes, until tender but still firm to the bite. Drain and stir into the turkey mixture with the parsley.

4 Spoon the mixture into an ovenproof dish, sprinkle with the breadcrumbs and remaining cheese and dot with the remaining butter. Bake in the preheated oven for 25 minutes until golden and bubbling. Serve immediately.

beef & macaroni soufflé

ingredients

serves 4

2 tbsp olive oil
1 large onion, chopped
225 g/8 oz fresh beef mince
1 garlic clove, finely chopped
400 g/14 oz canned chopped
    tomatoes
1 tbsp tomato purée
175 g/6 oz dried macaroni
butter, for greasing
3 eggs, separated
40 g/1½ oz freshly grated
    Parmesan cheese,
    plus extra to serve
salt and pepper

method

1 Preheat the oven to 190°C/375°F/Gas Mark 5. Heat the oil in a large heavy-based frying pan. Add the onion and cook over a low heat, stirring occasionally, for 5 minutes, or until softened. Add the beef and cook, breaking up the meat with a wooden spoon, until browned. Stir in the garlic, tomatoes and their can juices and tomato purée, then season to taste with salt and pepper. Bring to the boil, reduce the heat and simmer for 20 minutes, then remove the frying pan from the heat and leave to cool slightly.

2 Meanwhile, bring a large heavy-based saucepan of lightly salted water to the boil. Add the pasta, return to the boil and cook for 8–10 minutes, or until tender but still firm to the bite. Drain and reserve.

3 Lightly grease a 1.5-litre/2¾-pint soufflé dish with butter. Beat the egg yolks and add them to the meat sauce, then stir in the pasta. Whisk the egg whites until stiff peaks form, then fold into the pasta mixture. Spoon the mixture into the dish, sprinkle with the grated Parmesan cheese and bake in the preheated oven for 45 minutes, or until well risen and golden brown. Sprinkle with extra grated Parmesan cheese and serve immediately.

pasticcio

ingredients

serves 4

1 tbsp olive oil
1 onion, chopped
2 garlic cloves, finely chopped
450 g/1 lb fresh beef mince
2 tbsp tomato purée
2 tbsp plain flour
300 ml/10 fl oz chicken stock
1 tsp ground cinnamon
115 g/4 oz dried macaroni
2 beef tomatoes, sliced
300 ml/10 fl oz Greek-style yogurt
2 eggs, lightly beaten
salt and pepper

method

1 Preheat the oven to 190°C/375°F/Gas Mark 5. Heat the oil in a large heavy-based frying pan. Add the onion and garlic and cook over a low heat, stirring occasionally, for 5 minutes, or until softened. Add the mince and cook, breaking it up with a wooden spoon, until browned all over. Add the tomato purée and sprinkle in the flour. Cook, stirring, for 1 minute, then stir in the stock. Season to taste with salt and pepper and stir in the cinnamon. Bring to the boil, reduce the heat, cover and cook for 25 minutes.

2 Meanwhile, bring a large saucepan of lightly salted water to the boil. Add the pasta, bring back to the boil and cook for 8–10 minutes, until tender but still firm to the bite.

3 Drain the pasta and stir into the mince mixture. Spoon into a large ovenproof dish and arrange the tomato slices on top. Beat together the yogurt and eggs then spoon evenly over the mince. Bake the dish in the preheated oven for 1 hour until golden and bubbling. Serve immediately.

layered beef & feta bake

ingredients

serves 6

4 tbsp olive oil
1 onion, chopped
2 garlic cloves, finely chopped
650 g/1 lb 7 oz fresh beef mince
1½ tbsp tomato purée
600 g/1 lb 5 oz canned chopped
    tomatoes
2 tbsp Worcestershire sauce
1 tbsp chopped fresh oregano
750 g/1 lb 10 oz potatoes
2 aubergines, sliced
150 g/5½ oz feta cheese
600 ml/1 pint Greek-style yogurt
3 large eggs, lightly beaten
40 g/1½ oz Parmesan cheese,
    grated
salt and pepper

method

1 Heat half the oil in a large frying pan. Add the onion and garlic and cook over a low heat for 5 minutes, until softened. Add the beef, increase the heat to medium and cook, stirring frequently and breaking up the meat with a wooden spoon, for 8–10 minutes, until evenly browned. Drain off the fat. Stir in the tomato purée and cook for a further 2–3 minutes, then stir in the tomatoes, Worcestershire sauce and oregano. Season to taste with salt and pepper. Reduce the heat, cover and simmer for 30 minutes. Meanwhile, cook the potatoes in a saucepan of salted boiling water for 15 minutes. Drain and leave to cool slightly, then cut into thick slices.

2 Preheat the oven to 180°C/350°F/Gas Mark 4. Brush the aubergine slices with the remaining oil. Heat a large heavy-based frying pan. Add the aubergine slices, in batches, and cook over a medium heat for 3 minutes on each side, until softened. Drain on kitchen paper.

3 Transfer the beef mixture to an ovenproof dish and cover with the potato slices, followed by the aubergine slices. Crumble the feta over the top. Mix the yogurt, eggs and half the Parmesan in a bowl and pour over the dish. Sprinkle with the remaining Parmesan and bake in the preheated oven for 30–35 minutes, until golden brown. Serve immediately.

moussaka

ingredients

serves 4

2 aubergines, thinly sliced
450 g/1 lb fresh lean beef or
    lamb mince
2 onions, thinly sliced
1 tsp finely chopped garlic
400 g/14 oz canned tomatoes
2 tbsp chopped fresh parsley
2 eggs
300 ml/10 fl oz Greek-style yogurt
1 tbsp freshly grated Parmesan
    cheese
salt and pepper

method

1 Dry-fry the aubergine slices, in batches, in a non-stick
    frying pan on both sides until brown. Remove from
    the pan.

2 Add the beef to the frying pan and cook for 5 minutes,
    stirring, until evenly browned. Stir in the onions and
    garlic and cook for a further 5 minutes, or until brown.
    Add the tomatoes, parsley, and salt and pepper, then
    bring to the boil and simmer for 20 minutes, or until
    the meat is tender.

3 Preheat the oven to 180°C/350°F/Gas Mark 4. Arrange
    one-third of the aubergine slices in a layer in an
    ovenproof dish. Add half the meat mixture, then half
    the remaining aubergine slices. Add the remaining
    meat mixture and layer the remaining aubergine slices
    on top.

4 Beat the eggs in a bowl, then beat in the yogurt and
    add salt and pepper to taste. Pour the mixture over the
    aubergines and sprinkle the grated cheese on top.

5 Bake the moussaka in the preheated oven for
    45 minutes, or until golden brown. Serve straight
    from the dish.

cottage pie

ingredients

serves 6

650 g/1 lb 7 oz potatoes,
    cut into chunks
115 g/4 oz Cheddar cheese, grated
2 tbsp sunflower oil
1 onion, chopped
1 garlic clove, chopped
2 carrots, chopped
500 g/1 lb 2 oz fresh beef mince
115 g/4 oz mushrooms, sliced
300 ml/10 fl oz hot beef stock
1 tsp sugar
1 tbsp Worcestershire sauce
salt and pepper

method

1 Cook the potatoes in a large saucepan of salted boiling water for 20–25 minutes, until tender but not falling apart. Drain the potatoes, return to the pan and mash well, then stir in three-quarters of the cheese.

2 Meanwhile, heat the oil in a saucepan. Add the onion, garlic and carrots and cook over a low heat, stirring occasionally, for 5 minutes, until softened. Increase the heat to medium, add the beef and cook, stirring frequently and breaking it up with a wooden spoon, for 8–10 minutes, until evenly browned.

3 Add the mushrooms and cook for 2 minutes, then pour in the stock and stir in the sugar and Worcestershire sauce. Season to taste with salt and pepper. Reduce the heat, cover and simmer for 20 minutes.

4 Preheat the oven to 200°C/400°F/Gas Mark 6. Spoon the meat mixture into an ovenproof dish and spread the potato over the top. Sprinkle with the remaining cheese and bake in the preheated oven for 20 minutes, until the topping is golden brown. Serve immediately.

variation

Use 500 g/1 lb 2 oz lamb mince instead of beef, omit the mushrooms and substitute 2 tablespoons of tomato purée for the sugar to make a classic shepherd's pie.

beef 'n' beans

ingredients

serves 4

1 onion, chopped
500 g/1 lb 2 oz fresh beef mince
400 g/14 oz canned baked beans
1 tbsp maple syrup
1 tbsp mild mustard
1 tbsp concentrated beef stock
650 g/1 lb 7 oz potatoes, diced
115 g/4 oz cream cheese
salt and pepper

method

1 Put the onion and beef into a large non-stick frying pan and cook over a medium heat, stirring frequently and breaking up the meat with a wooden spoon, for 8–10 minutes, until evenly browned.

2 Stir the baked beans, maple syrup, mustard and concentrated stock into the frying pan and season to taste with pepper. Reduce the heat, cover and simmer, stirring occasionally and adding a little water if the mixture seems to be drying out, for 15 minutes.

3 Meanwhile, cook the potatoes in a saucepan of salted boiling water for 20 minutes, until tender but not falling apart. Drain the potatoes and return to the pan. Add the cream cheese, season to taste with salt and pepper and mash until smooth.

4 Preheat the grill. Transfer the beef mixture to an ovenproof dish and spread the mashed potato over the top. Cook under the preheated grill for 5 minutes, until the topping is golden brown. Serve immediately.

beef with garlic potatoes

ingredients

serves 4

500 g/1 lb 2 oz potatoes
3 tbsp olive oil
1 onion, chopped
500 g/1 lb 2 oz fresh beef mince
225 g/8 oz carrots, chopped
4 tomatoes, peeled and chopped
1 tsp cornflour
300 ml/10 fl oz hot beef stock
1 tbsp chopped fresh parsley
1 tsp chopped fresh sage
3 garlic cloves, very finely chopped
salt and pepper

method

1 Preheat the oven to 180°C/350°F/Gas Mark 4. Parboil the potatoes in a saucepan of salted boiling water for 15 minutes, then drain and leave to cool.

2 Meanwhile, heat 1 tablespoon of the oil in a large saucepan. Add the onion and cook over a low heat, stirring occasionally, for 5 minutes, until softened.

3 Add the beef, increase the heat to medium and cook, stirring frequently and breaking it up with a wooden spoon, for 8–10 minutes, until evenly browned. Add the carrots and tomatoes. Stir the cornflour into the stock, then stir the mixture into the pan. Season to taste with salt and pepper. Stir in the parsley and sage and bring to the boil, then reduce the heat and simmer for 5 minutes.

4 Meanwhile, cut the potatoes into slices. Mix together the garlic and the remaining oil in a small bowl and season to taste with salt and pepper.

5 Transfer the beef mixture to an ovenproof dish and arrange the potato slices on top. Brush the garlic-flavoured oil over them and bake in the preheated oven for 30–35 minutes, until the topping is golden brown. Serve immediately.

baked beef & potato layers

ingredients

serves 4

55 g/2 oz tomato purée
125 ml/4 fl oz water
400 g/14 oz canned chopped
    tomatoes
1 tbsp chopped fresh thyme
500 g/1 lb 2 oz potatoes
40 g/1½ oz butter, plus extra
    for greasing
225 g/8 oz fresh beef mince
1 egg, lightly beaten
2 onions, sliced
115 g/4 oz Cheddar cheese, grated
salt and pepper

method

1 Heat the tomato purée, water, tomatoes and thyme
   in a saucepan. Season to taste with salt and pepper.
   Bring to the boil, then reduce the heat and simmer,
   stirring occasionally, for 30 minutes, until thickened.
   Meanwhile, cook the potatoes in a saucepan of salted
   boiling water for 15 minutes. Drain and leave to cool
   slightly, then cut into 5-mm/¼-inch slices.

2 Preheat the oven to 180°C/350°F/Gas Mark 4. Grease an
   ovenproof dish with butter.

3 Mix together the beef and egg in a bowl and season to
   taste with salt and pepper. Divide the mixture into 6
   portions and shape each into a patty about 5 mm/
   ¼ inch thick. Melt 25 g/1 oz of the butter in a frying
   pan. Add the patties and cook over a medium heat for
   3 minutes on each side, until lightly browned. Remove
   with a fish slice. Add the onions to the frying pan and
   cook over a low heat for 5 minutes, until softened.

4 Put half the potato slices in the base of the prepared
   dish. Cover with the beef patties, then the onions and
   sprinkle with half the cheese. Top with the remaining
   potato slices and pour over the tomato mixture.
   Sprinkle with the remaining cheese, dot with the
   remaining butter and bake in the preheated oven for
   20 minutes. Serve immediately.

beef & cheese cobbler

ingredients

serves 4

2 tbsp sunflower oil
500 g/1 lb 2 oz fresh beef
    mince
2 tbsp plain flour
500 g/1 lb 2 oz onions,
    cut into wedges
2 tbsp tomato ketchup
1 tbsp chopped fresh thyme
1 bay leaf
300 ml/10 fl oz beef stock
salt and pepper

cobbler topping

225 g/8 oz self-raising flour,
    plus extra for dusting
½ tsp mustard powder
pinch of salt
40 g/1½ oz butter,
    cut into small pieces
85 g/3 oz Cheddar cheese,
    grated
dash of Tabasco sauce
milk, for glazing

method

1 Preheat the oven to 180°C/350°F/Gas Mark 4. Heat the oil in a frying pan. Add the beef and cook over a medium heat, stirring frequently and breaking it up with a wooden spoon, for 8–10 minutes, until the mince is evenly browned.

2 Spoon the beef into a casserole, then stir in the plain flour. Add the onions, tomato ketchup, thyme and bay leaf and season to taste with salt and pepper. Pour in the stock and stir well, then cover and bake in the preheated oven for 1 hour.

3 Meanwhile, sift the self-raising flour, mustard powder and salt into a bowl. Add the butter and rub it in with your fingertips until the mixture resembles breadcrumbs. Stir in the cheese, Tabasco sauce and enough water to mix to a soft dough.

4 Roll out the dough to a thickness of 1 cm/½ inch on a lightly floured surface, then stamp out rounds with a 6-cm/2½-inch fluted round cutter.

5 Remove the casserole from the oven and take off the lid. Remove and discard the bay leaf. Cover the beef mixture with the dough rounds and brush them with milk. Return the casserole, without the lid, to the oven and bake for a further 35 minutes, until the topping is golden brown. Serve immediately.

beef & vegetable gratin

ingredients

serves 6–8

3 tbsp sunflower oil

2 garlic cloves, finely chopped

2 onions, sliced

1 kg/2 lb 4 oz fresh beef mince

500 g/1 lb 2 oz courgettes,
    thinly sliced

300 g/10½ oz carrots,
    thinly sliced

1 red pepper, deseeded and
    thinly sliced

55 g/2 oz raisins

85 g/3 oz butter

85 g/3 oz plain flour

850 ml/1½ pints milk

115 g/4 oz Cheddar cheese,
    grated

350 g/12 oz canned sweetcorn,
    drained

400 g/14 oz canned cannellini
    beans, drained and rinsed

2 tbsp chopped fresh parsley

4 egg yolks

salt and pepper

method

1 Heat the oil in a large saucepan. Add the garlic and onions and cook over a low heat, stirring occasionally, for 5 minutes, until softened. Add the beef, increase the heat to medium and cook, stirring frequently and breaking it up with a wooden spoon, for 8–10 minutes, until evenly browned. Stir in the courgettes, carrots, red pepper and raisins and season to taste with salt and pepper. Reduce the heat, cover and simmer for 25 minutes.

2 Meanwhile, preheat the oven to 180°C/350°F/Gas Mark 4. Melt the butter in a saucepan. Add the flour and cook over a low heat, stirring constantly, for 2 minutes. Gradually stir in the milk, a little at a time, until smooth and thickened. Remove the pan from the heat and stir in the cheese until melted.

3 Stir the sweetcorn, beans and parsley into the beef mixture and simmer for a further 3 minutes, then remove the pan from the heat. Spoon the mixture into an ovenproof dish.

4 Lightly beat the egg yolks in a bowl with a fork, then stir in 4 tablespoons of the cheese sauce. Stir the egg yolk mixture into the cheese sauce and pour it over the meat mixture to cover. Bake in the preheated oven for 25–30 minutes, until the topping is golden brown. Serve immediately.

upside-down pie

ingredients

serves 4

3 tbsp sunflower oil
2 onions, finely chopped
1 garlic clove, finely chopped
350 g/12 oz fresh beef mince
55 g/2 oz mushrooms,
   finely chopped
4 tomatoes, peeled and diced
½ tsp anchovy paste
1 tbsp Worcestershire sauce
1 tsp dried oregano
1 bay leaf
150 ml/5 fl oz beef stock
150 ml/5 fl oz red wine
salt and pepper

pastry

175 g/6 oz self-raising flour
pinch of salt
55 g/2 oz butter,
   cut into small pieces
85 g/3 oz Cheddar cheese,
   grated
1 egg yolk
100–150 ml/3½–5 fl oz milk

method

1 Heat the oil in a saucepan. Add the onions and garlic and cook over a low heat, stirring occasionally, for 5 minutes, until softened. Add the beef, increase the heat to medium and cook, stirring frequently and breaking it up with a wooden spoon, for 8–10 minutes, until evenly browned.

2 Add the mushrooms and tomatoes and cook for a further 3 minutes, then stir in the anchovy paste, Worcestershire sauce, oregano, bay leaf, stock and wine. Season to taste with salt and pepper. Bring to the boil, then reduce the heat and simmer, stirring occasionally, for 20 minutes.

3 Meanwhile, preheat the oven to 180°C/350°F/Gas Mark 4. Sift the flour and salt into a bowl. Add the butter and rub it in with your fingertips until the mixture resembles breadcrumbs. Stir in the cheese, then add the egg yolk and enough of the milk to mix to a soft dough. Shape the dough into a 20-cm/8-inch round.

4 Transfer the beef mixture to a 20-cm/8-inch round cake tin and put the dough round on top. Bake in the preheated oven for 50 minutes, until the topping is golden brown. Remove the tin from the oven and invert onto a warmed serving dish. Cut into wedges and serve immediately.

minced beef casserole

ingredients

serves 6

6 tbsp olive oil, plus extra
    if needed
1 kg/2 lb 4 oz fresh beef mince
6 spring onions, chopped
6 tomatoes, peeled and chopped
1 red pepper, deseeded and sliced
2 slices fresh pineapple
    (about 2 cm/¾ inch thick),
    peeled, cored and chopped
1 tbsp chopped fresh thyme
2 aubergines, thinly sliced
175 g/6 oz Cheddar cheese,
    grated
salt and pepper

method

1 Heat 2 tablespoons of the oil in a large frying pan.
   Add the beef and cook over a medium heat, stirring
   frequently and breaking it up with a wooden spoon, for
   8–10 minutes, until lightly browned. Stir in the spring
   onions, tomatoes, red pepper and pineapple and cook,
   stirring occasionally, for a further 5 minutes. Stir in the
   thyme and season to taste with salt and pepper.
   Reduce the heat and simmer, stirring occasionally, for
   15 minutes.

2 Preheat the oven to 180°C/350°F/Gas Mark 4. Heat the
   remaining oil in a frying pan. Add the aubergine slices,
   in batches, and cook for 2–3 minutes on each side, until
   softened. Add more oil to the pan as required. Remove
   the aubergine slices from the pan and drain them on
   kitchen paper.

3 Put one-third of the aubergine slices in an ovenproof
   dish and add half the beef mixture. Add half the
   remaining aubergine slices and top with the remaining
   beef mixture. Cover with the remaining aubergine
   slices, sprinkle with the cheese and bake in the
   preheated oven for 30 minutes, until the topping is
   golden brown. Serve immediately.

beef goulash

ingredients

serves 6

1 tbsp olive oil
500 g/1 lb 2 oz fresh
    lean beef mince
2 onions, finely chopped
2 garlic cloves, finely chopped
2 tbsp plain flour
225 ml/8 fl oz water
400 g/14 oz canned chopped
    tomatoes
1 carrot, finely chopped
225 g/8 oz red pepper, roasted,
    peeled, deseeded and chopped
1 tsp Hungarian paprika
¼ tsp caraway seeds
pinch of dried oregano
1 litre/1¾ pints beef stock
55 g/2 oz dried tagliatelle,
    broken into small pieces
salt and pepper
soured cream and sprigs of fresh
    coriander, to garnish

method

1 Preheat the oven to 160°C/325°F/Gas Mark 3. Heat the oil in a large flameproof casserole dish over a medium–high heat. Add the beef and sprinkle with salt and pepper. Fry until lightly browned.

2 Reduce the heat and add the onions and garlic. Cook for about 3 minutes, stirring frequently, until the onions are softened. Stir in the flour and continue cooking for 1 minute.

3 Add the water and stir to combine well, scraping the bottom of the pan to mix in the flour. Stir in the tomatoes, carrot, pepper, paprika, caraway seeds, oregano and stock.

4 Cover and cook in the preheated oven for 1 hour, until all the vegetables are tender.

5 Meanwhile, bring a large saucepan of salted water to the boil. Add the pasta, return to the boil and cook for 8–10 minutes, until tender but still firm to the bite. Drain and stir into the goulash.

6 Taste and adjust the seasoning, if necessary. Ladle into warmed bowls and top each with a tablespoonful of soured cream. Garnish with coriander and serve.

something spicy

turkey & chorizo empanadas

ingredients

serves 8

2 tbsp vegetable oil,
plus extra for greasing
1 onion, finely chopped
2 garlic cloves, finely chopped
250 g/9 oz fresh turkey mince
50 g/1¾ oz chorizo sausage,
finely chopped
2 tsp smoked paprika
1 yellow pepper, deseeded and
finely chopped
70 g/2½ oz frozen peas
2 tbsp fresh flat-leaf parsley,
finely chopped
500 g/1 lb 2 oz ready-made
shortcrust pastry
1 small egg, beaten
salt and pepper

method

1 Preheat the oven to 180°C/350°F/Gas Mark 4. Heat
the oil in a non-stick frying pan, add the onion and
cook for 4–5 minutes, until softened. Add the garlic and
cook for a further 1 minute.

2 Add the mince, chorizo, paprika and yellow pepper and
continue to cook for a further 6–8 minutes, until the
mince is evenly browned. Stir in the peas, parsley, and
salt and pepper to taste.

3 Roll out the pastry on a lightly floured work surface
and use a saucer to cut out 8 rounds. Spoon a small
amount of the filling onto one half of each round. Use
a pastry brush to brush the edges of the pastry with a
little beaten egg and fold the rounds in half over the
filling, crimping the edges to form a tight seal.

4 Lightly grease a baking tray with oil. Place the
empanadas on the prepared tray and brush each
one with the remaining beaten egg. Bake in the
preheated oven for 15–18 minutes until golden.
Serve immediately.

quesadillas

ingredients

serves 4

500 g/1 lb 2 oz fresh beef mince
1 onion, finely chopped
1 red pepper, deseeded and
    finely chopped
1 garlic clove, crushed
1 tsp smoked paprika
½ tsp cumin seeds
½ fresh red chilli, deseeded and
    finely chopped
4 tbsp tomato purée
400 g/14 oz canned red kidney
    beans, drained and rinsed
vegetable oil spray
8 flour tortillas
85 g/3 oz Cheddar cheese, grated
salt and pepper
tomato salsa, to serve

method

1 Dry-fry the mince in a non-stick frying pan for
4–5 minutes, until starting to brown.

2 Add the onion, red pepper and garlic and cook for a
further 1–2 minutes. Add the paprika, cumin seeds and
chilli and cook for 1 minute. Add the tomato purée,
beans, and salt and pepper to taste. Cover and cook for
10 minutes, until the meat is thoroughly cooked.

3 Preheat the oven to 140°C/275°F/Gas Mark 1. Heat a
non-stick frying pan over a medium heat and spray
with the oil. Place a tortilla in the pan and spoon over
about one-quarter of the meat mixture, spreading it
across the surface of the tortilla. Scatter over some
cheese, top with another tortilla and press down.
Fry for 1–2 minutes, then tip onto a plate and slide
back into the pan to cook the other side for a further
1–2 minutes. Transfer to a baking tray, cover and place
in the preheated oven to keep warm while cooking the
remaining tortillas.

4 Serve the warm quesadillas cut into quarters with
some tomato salsa.

beef enchiladas

ingredients

serves 4

500 g/1 lb 2 oz fresh beef mince
1 onion, finely chopped
2 garlic cloves, finely chopped
1 tbsp cumin seeds
1 tsp ground cinnamon
2 tsp hot chilli powder
1 tsp ground coriander
2 tbsp tomato purée
400 g/14 oz canned chopped
  tomatoes
100 ml/3½ fl oz red wine
100 ml/3½ fl oz water
8 small flour tortillas
55 g/2 oz Cheddar cheese, grated
salt and pepper

to serve

sour cream
guacamole

method

1 Dry-fry the mince in a non-stick frying pan for
  4–5 minutes, until starting to brown. Add the onion
  and garlic and cook for a further 1–2 minutes.

2 Add the cumin seeds, cinnamon, chilli powder and
  coriander and cook, stirring constantly, for 1–2 minutes,
  until the spices are lightly toasted. Stir in the tomato
  purée and cook for a further 1 minute.

3 Add half the tomatoes, the red wine, water, and salt
  and pepper to taste. Stir well, cover and simmer for
  10 minutes, until the beef is thoroughly cooked.

4 Preheat the oven to 180°C/350°F/Gas Mark 4. Spoon
  some of the chilli filling in a line down the centre
  of each tortilla and fold in the ends and sides to
  form a parcel.

5 Place the enchiladas seam side down in an ovenproof
  dish and spoon over the remaining chopped tomatoes.
  Scatter over the cheese and bake in the oven for
  10 minutes, until the cheese is just golden.

6 Serve immediately, accompanied by the sour cream
  and guacamole.

beef burritos

ingredients

serves 4

500 g/1 lb 2 oz fresh beef mince
1 onion, finely chopped
1 yellow pepper, deseeded and
    finely chopped
1 garlic clove, crushed
½ tsp cumin seeds
1 tsp dried oregano
1 fresh red chilli, deseeded and
    finely chopped
4 tbsp tomato purée
400 g/14 oz canned red kidney
    beans, drained and rinsed
8 large flour tortillas
vegetable oil spray
4 tbsp grated Cheddar cheese
salt and pepper
tomato salsa, to serve

method

1 Dry-fry the mince in a non-stick frying pan for
    4–5 minutes, until starting to brown.

2 Add the onion, yellow pepper and garlic and cook for
    a further 1–2 minutes. Add the cumin seeds, oregano,
    chilli, tomato purée, beans, and salt and pepper to
    taste. Cover and cook for 10 minutes, until the meat
    is thoroughly cooked.

3 Warm the tortillas in a frying pan, sprayed with oil, over
    a medium heat. Fill the tortillas with the mince mixture,
    scatter over the cheese, wrap to form a parcel and
    serve with tomato salsa.

beef tacos

ingredients

serves 4

500 g/1 lb 2 oz fresh beef mince
1 onion, finely chopped
1 yellow pepper, deseeded and
    finely chopped
1 garlic clove crushed
1 tsp smoked paprika
½ tsp cumin seeds
1 fresh red chilli, deseeded and
    finely chopped
4 tbsp tomato purée
salt and pepper

to serve

taco shells
shredded iceberg lettuce
grated Cheddar cheese
sour cream
chopped avocado

method

1 Dry-fry the mince in a non-stick frying pan for
   4–5 minutes, until lightly browned.

2 Add the onion, yellow pepper and garlic and cook for a
   further 1–2 minutes. Add the paprika, cumin seeds and
   chilli and cook for 1 minute. Add the tomato purée, and
   salt and pepper to taste, cover and cook for 10 minutes,
   until the meat is thoroughly cooked.

3 Warm the taco shells according to the packet
   instructions. Spoon the spicy meat mixture into the
   shells and serve topped with lettuce, cheese, sour
   cream and avocado.

variation

Use 500 g/1 lb 2 oz chicken mince instead of beef. Omit
the smoked paprika and cumin. After adding the salt and
pepper, add 400 g/14 oz canned chopped tomatoes and
125 g/4 oz canned kidney beans, drained. Bring to the
boil. Reduce the heat to medium–low, cover and cook for
10 minutes. Serve in taco shells.

beef with pimientos

ingredients

serves 4

2 tbsp olive oil
3 large onions,
    thinly sliced into rings
2 garlic cloves, finely chopped
650 g/1 lb 7 oz fresh beef mince
2 tbsp Worcestershire sauce
3 tbsp lemon juice
1 tsp hot paprika
1 tbsp light brown sugar
115 g/4 oz canned or bottled
    pimientos, drained and
    sliced lengthways
salt and pepper

method

1 Heat the oil in a large frying pan. Add the onions and garlic and cook over a low heat, stirring occasionally, for 5 minutes, until softened. Add the beef, increase the heat to medium and cook, stirring frequently and breaking up the meat with a wooden spoon, for 8–10 minutes, until evenly browned.

2 Stir in the Worcestershire sauce, lemon juice, paprika and sugar. Season to taste with salt and pepper, then cook, stirring frequently, for 5 minutes. Add the pimientos, reduce the heat and simmer, stirring occasionally, for 20 minutes, until the meat is cooked through and tender. Serve immediately.

stir-fried beef

ingredients

serves 6

6 tbsp Chinese rice wine or
   dry sherry
3 garlic cloves,
   very finely chopped
2 tbsp finely chopped
   fresh ginger
1 tbsp dark soy sauce
1 tsp sesame oil
1 tbsp cornflour
900 g/2 lb fresh beef mince
3 tbsp groundnut oil
2 tbsp hoisin sauce
2 tbsp oyster sauce
2 tsp rice vinegar
2 carrots, thinly sliced
   diagonally
4 spring onions, thinly sliced
   lengthways
225 g/8 oz broccoli florets
1 large red pepper, deseeded
   and thinly sliced
175 g/6 oz baby corn,
   halved lengthways

method

1 Mix together half the rice wine, the garlic, ginger, soy sauce, sesame oil and cornflour in a bowl. Add the beef, turning and stirring to coat, cover with clingfilm and leave to marinate in the refrigerator for 1 hour.

2 Heat a wok over a medium heat, then add the groundnut oil, swirl it around the wok and heat. Remove the beef from the bowl, add it to the wok and stir-fry, breaking it up with a wooden spoon, for 3–5 minutes, until evenly browned.

3 Stir in the remaining rice wine, the hoisin sauce, oyster sauce and vinegar and cook, stirring constantly, for 1 minute.

4 Stir in the carrots, spring onions, broccoli, red pepper and baby corn and stir-fry for a further 3–4 minutes, until the vegetables are just tender. Serve immediately.

beef soup with ginger & lemon grass

ingredients

serves 6

15 g/¹/₂ oz dried thread noodles
225 g/8 oz fresh beef mince
    (preferably freshly ground
    sirloin steak)
2 shallots, finely chopped
4 tbsp Thai fish sauce
2 tbsp groundnut oil
85 g/3 oz long-grain rice
1 tsp grated fresh ginger
1.5 litres/2³/₄ pints water
1 tbsp brown sugar
2 garlic cloves, very finely
    chopped
1 tbsp very finely chopped
    lemon grass
2 tbsp crushed unsalted
    roasted peanuts
2 spring onions, thinly sliced
1 tbsp chopped fresh coriander
salt and pepper

method

1 Soak the noodles in enough lukewarm water to cover for 15 minutes, or cook according to the packet instructions, until soft. Drain and cut into 5-cm/2-inch lengths.

2 Put the beef, shallots and 1 tablespoon of the fish sauce into a large bowl, season to taste with pepper and mix well. Cover with clingfilm and chill in the refrigerator until required.

3 Heat half the oil in a large saucepan. Add the rice and ginger and cook over a low heat, stirring constantly, for 1 minute. Pour in the water, increase the heat to medium and bring to the boil. Partially cover the pan, reduce the heat and simmer for 20 minutes, until the rice is tender. Stir in the sugar and the remaining fish sauce and season to taste with salt.

4 Heat the remaining oil in a small frying pan. Add the garlic and lemon grass and cook over a low–medium heat, stirring constantly, for 1 minute, then stir into the rice mixture with the noodles and the beef mixture. Bring back to the boil, stirring constantly and breaking up the meat with a wooden spoon. Pour into warmed soup bowls and sprinkle with the peanuts, spring onions and coriander. Serve immediately.

ants climbing a tree

ingredients

serves 4

250 g/9 oz thick rice noodles
1 tbsp cornflour
3 tbsp soy sauce
1½ tbsp Chinese rice wine
1½ tsp sugar
1½ tsp sesame oil
350 g/12 oz fresh lean beef mince
1½ tbsp groundnut oil
2 large garlic cloves,
    finely chopped
1 large fresh red chilli, or to taste,
    deseeded and thinly sliced
3 spring onions, finely chopped
finely chopped fresh coriander,
    to garnish

method

1 Soak the noodles in enough lukewarm water to cover for 15 minutes, or cook according to the packet instructions, until soft. Drain well and set aside.

2 Meanwhile, put the cornflour in a separate large bowl, then stir in the soy sauce, rice wine, sugar and sesame oil, stirring until smooth. Add the mince and use your hands to toss the ingredients together without squeezing the beef. Set aside to marinate for 10 minutes.

3 Heat a wok over a high heat, then add the groundnut oil. Add the garlic, chilli and spring onions and stir around for about 30 seconds. Tip in the mince together with any marinade left in the bowl and stir-fry for about 5 minutes, or until the beef is no longer pink. Add the noodles and use 2 forks to mix together. Sprinkle with the chopped coriander and serve.

beef with red pepper, fruit & nuts

ingredients

serves 4

3 tbsp sunflower oil

2 onions, finely chopped

2 garlic cloves, finely chopped

2 celery sticks, chopped

1 red pepper,
deseeded and chopped

1 kg/2 lb 4 oz fresh beef mince

400 g/14 oz canned chopped
tomatoes

400 g/14 oz canned haricot beans,
drained and rinsed

6 tbsp tomato purée

1 tsp chilli powder

½ tsp ground nutmeg

2 Bramley apples, cored and
chopped

55 g/2 oz ready-to-eat dried
apricots, chopped

2 tbsp slivered almonds,
plus extra to garnish

115 g/4 oz frozen French beans,
thawed

salt and pepper

method

1 Heat the oil in a large frying pan. Add the onions, garlic, celery and red pepper and cook over a low heat, stirring occasionally, for 5 minutes, until softened. Add the beef, increase the heat to medium and cook, stirring frequently and breaking it up with a wooden spoon, for 8–10 minutes, until evenly browned.

2 Add the tomatoes, haricot beans, tomato purée, chilli powder, nutmeg, apples, apricots, almonds and French beans. Season to taste with salt and pepper. Reduce the heat, cover and simmer for 30 minutes, then remove the lid and simmer for a further 10 minutes.

3 Serve immediately, garnished with slivered almonds.

thai chicken cakes

ingredients

serves 4

½ bunch spring onions, trimmed
    and roughly chopped
3-cm/1¼-inch piece fresh ginger,
    roughly chopped
3 garlic cloves, crushed
handful fresh coriander,
    including the stalks
1 red chilli, deseeded and
    roughly chopped
500 g/1 lb 2 oz fresh chicken mince
2 tbsp light soy sauce
dash nam pla (Thai fish sauce)
1 egg white
2 tbsp plain flour
finely grated zest of 1 lime
2–3 tbsp vegetable oil, for frying
pepper
lime wedges and sweet chilli
    sauce, to serve

method

1 Place the spring onions, ginger, garlic, coriander and chilli in a food processor or blender and process until everything is finely chopped.

2 Tip into a mixing bowl, add the chicken and combine together with the soy sauce, nam pla, egg white, flour, lime zest and black pepper.

3 Heat a little oil in a non-stick frying pan and add spoonfuls of the mixture in batches. Cook each batch for about 4 minutes on each side, until golden and cooked through. Transfer to a plate and keep warm while cooking the remaining mixture.

4 Serve the cooked Thai chicken cakes with lime wedges and sweet chilli sauce for dipping.

stuffed peppers

ingredients

serves 4

4 large red peppers

3 tbsp sunflower oil,
    plus extra for brushing

2 onions, finely chopped

2 garlic cloves, finely chopped

2 fresh green chillies, deseeded
    and finely chopped

500 g/1 lb 2 oz fresh beef mince

1 tsp Tabasco sauce

2 tbsp plain flour

225 ml/8 fl oz beef stock

150 ml/5 fl oz single cream

225 g/8 oz cream cheese

pinch of cayenne pepper

115 g/4 oz sultanas

salt

method

1 Cut off the tops of the peppers, remove the seeds and
    membranes, then set aside. Cut out the stems from the
    sliced tops and chop the flesh.

2 Heat the oil in a frying pan. Add the onions, garlic,
    chillies and chopped pepper and cook over a low heat,
    stirring occasionally, for 5 minutes, until softened. Add
    the beef and Tabasco and season to taste with salt.
    Increase the heat to medium and cook, stirring
    frequently and breaking up the meat with a wooden
    spoon, for 8–10 minutes, until evenly browned. Stir in
    the flour, then gradually stir in the stock. Bring to the
    boil, stirring constantly, then reduce the heat, cover
    and simmer for 30 minutes.

3 Preheat the oven to 180°C/350°F/Gas Mark 4. Brush an
    ovenproof dish with oil. Spoon the beef mixture into
    the peppers. Stand them upright in the prepared dish
    and bake in the preheated oven for 45 minutes.

4 Put the cream, cream cheese and cayenne pepper into a
    saucepan, season to taste with salt and stir until smooth.
    Add the sultanas and cook over a medium heat, stirring
    constantly, until hot. Do not allow the mixture to boil.

5 Remove the peppers from the oven and pour the
    cream cheese sauce over them. Return to the oven and
    bake for a further 15 minutes. Serve immediately.

minced beef hash

ingredients

serves 2

450 g/1 lb potatoes,
    cut into chunks
350 g/12 oz fresh beef mince
1 red pepper, deseeded and
    finely chopped
½ tsp sweet paprika
1 tbsp chopped fresh parsley,
    plus extra to garnish
3 tbsp sunflower oil
1 onion, finely chopped
2 eggs
salt and pepper

method

1 Cook the potatoes in a saucepan of salted boiling water
   for 20–25 minutes, until tender but not falling apart.
   Drain and leave to cool.

2 Meanwhile, mix together the beef, red pepper, paprika
   and parsley in a bowl. Season to taste with salt and
   pepper. Dice the potatoes and add them to the
   mixture, stirring gently until thoroughly combined.

3 Heat the oil in a large frying pan. Add the onion
   and cook over a low heat, stirring occasionally, for
   5 minutes, until softened.

4 Add the beef mixture to the pan and shake the pan to
   mix it with the onion, then press down gently with a
   wooden spoon. Cook over a medium heat, without
   stirring, for 5 minutes, until browned on the underside.
   Stir well, then cook, without stirring, for 5 minutes.
   Repeat the stirring and cooking twice more until the
   mixture is evenly browned.

5 Reduce the heat. Make 2 hollows in the mixture with
   the back of a spoon. Crack an egg into each hollow,
   cover and cook for a further 5 minutes, until the whites
   have set. Cut the hash into halves, each containing an
   egg, garnish with parsley and serve immediately.

moroccan-style mince

ingredients

serves 4

2 tbsp vegetable oil
1 large onion, finely chopped
2 garlic cloves, finely chopped
1 tbsp ground cumin
1 tsp ground cinnamon
2 tsp ground turmeric
500 g/1 lb 2oz fresh chicken mince
500 ml/18 fl oz chicken stock
70 g/2½ oz raisins
250 g/9 oz couscous
finely grated zest and juice
    of 1 lemon
30 g/1 oz toasted pine kernels
salt and pepper
fresh sprigs of flat-leaf parsley,
    to garnish

method

1 Heat the oil in a large, non-stick frying pan, add the onion and cook over a low heat, stirring occasionally, for 4–5 minutes, until softened. Add the garlic and spices and cook for a further 1 minute over a medium heat.

2 Add the mince and cook, stirring frequently and breaking up the meat with a wooden spoon, for 4–5 minutes, until lightly browned. Add the stock and raisins, cover and cook over a low heat for a further 8–10 minutes.

3 Add the couscous, and salt and pepper to taste, stir and cover again. Simmer for 5–6 minutes, until the couscous has absorbed the stock and is fully cooked.

4 Remove from the heat, then stir in the lemon zest and juice and pine kernels. Garnish with parsley and serve immediately.

spiced beef & pistachio nuts

ingredients

serves 4

55 g/2 oz butter
1 Spanish onion, chopped
2 garlic cloves, chopped
3 fresh green chillies,
    deseeded and chopped
1 kg/2 lb 4 oz fresh beef mince
2 tbsp roughly chopped pistachio
    nuts, plus extra to garnish
1½ tbsp garam masala
4 tomatoes, peeled and diced
4 tbsp fresh breadcrumbs
4 tbsp soured cream
salt and pepper

method

1 Preheat the oven to 190°C/375°F/Gas Mark 5. Melt the butter in a saucepan. Add the onion, garlic and chillies and cook over a low heat, stirring occasionally, for 5 minutes, until softened. Add the beef, increase the heat to medium and cook, stirring frequently and breaking it up with a wooden spoon, for 8–10 minutes, until evenly browned.

2 Remove the pan from the heat, stir in the pistachio nuts, garam masala, tomatoes, breadcrumbs and soured cream and season to taste with salt and pepper. Mix well until thoroughly combined, then spoon the mixture into an ovenproof dish.

3 Bake in the preheated oven for 35–45 minutes, until the top is lightly browned. Serve immediately, garnished with pistachio nuts.

masala keema (spicy beef mince)

ingredients

serves 4

500 g/1 lb 2 oz fresh beef mince
1 large onion, finely chopped
2 garlic cloves, crushed
2 potatoes, diced
1 tsp cumin seeds
2 tsp hot chilli powder
1 tsp turmeric
1 tsp ground coriander
2 tsp garam masala
400 g/14 oz canned chopped
    tomatoes
125 g/4½ oz frozen peas
salt and pepper

to serve

2 tbsp natural yogurt
fresh sprig of coriander
naan breads

method

1 Dry-fry the mince in a non-stick covered frying pan for
4–5 minutes, until browned.

2 Add the onion, garlic and potatoes and fry for a further
1–2 minutes. Add the cumin seeds, chilli powder,
turmeric, coriander and garam masala and cook,
stirring constantly, for a further 1–2 minutes.

3 Add the tomatoes, and salt and pepper to taste, cover
and simmer for 10–12 minutes, until the potatoes
are tender.

4 Add the peas and cook for a further 1–2 minutes.
Spoon over the yogurt, garnish with the coriander and
serve with naan breads.

beef curry

ingredients

serves 4

4 tbsp groundnut oil
1 large onion, finely chopped
1 green pepper,
    deseeded and diced
1 tsp cumin seeds
4 green cardamom pods
2 bay leaves
500 g/1 lb 2 oz tomatoes,
    peeled and chopped
2 garlic cloves, finely chopped
450 g/1 lb fresh beef mince
2 tsp ground coriander
2 tsp ground turmeric
1 tsp chilli powder
600 ml/1 pint beef stock
2 tbsp chopped fresh coriander
salt
cooked rice and naan bread,
    to serve

method

1 Heat half the oil in a large saucepan. Add the onion, green pepper, cumin seeds, cardamom pods and bay leaves and cook over a low heat, stirring constantly, for 2–3 minutes, until the spices give off their aroma. Add the tomatoes and cook, stirring frequently, for 10 minutes.

2 Meanwhile, heat the remaining oil in a frying pan. Add the garlic and cook, stirring frequently, for 1 minute, then add the beef, ground coriander, turmeric and chilli powder. Cook over a medium heat, stirring constantly and breaking up the meat with a wooden spoon, for 4–5 minutes, until the meat is evenly browned. Transfer the mixture to the saucepan.

3 Pour in the stock and bring to the boil, then reduce the heat, cover and simmer, stirring occasionally, for 20–25 minutes. If the mixture seems to be drying out, add a little water.

4 Remove and discard the bay leaves and cardamom pods, then season to taste with salt. Scatter over the chopped coriander and serve immediately with rice and naan bread.

balti beef curry

ingredients

serves 4

3 tbsp corn oil
4 onions, thinly sliced
2 garlic cloves, finely chopped
2.5-cm/1-inch piece fresh
    ginger, finely chopped
1 tsp ground coriander
1 tsp chilli powder
1 tsp ground turmeric
650 g/1 lb 7 oz fresh beef
    mince
200 g/7 oz canned chopped
    tomatoes
2 tbsp chopped fresh coriander
salt
cooked rice, to serve

method

1 Heat the oil in a frying pan. Add the onions, garlic and ginger and cook over a low heat, stirring occasionally, for 5 minutes, until softened. Add the ground coriander, chilli powder and turmeric and cook, stirring occasionally, for a further 3 minutes.

2 Add the beef, increase the heat to medium and cook, stirring frequently and breaking it up with a wooden spoon, for 8–10 minutes, until evenly browned. Stir in the tomatoes and season to taste with salt. Reduce the heat, cover and simmer, stirring occasionally, for 15 minutes. Uncover the pan and cook for a further 5 minutes.

3 Taste and adjust the seasoning, adding more salt if needed. Transfer the curry to a warmed serving dish, sprinkle with the chopped coriander and serve immediately with rice.

spicy beef & sweet potatoes

ingredients

serves 4

4 sweet potatoes
800 g/1 lb 12 oz canned
    chopped tomatoes
2 fresh green chillies,
    deseeded and chopped
6 black peppercorns
6 allspice berries
1 cinnamon stick
1 tsp ground coriander
2 tbsp sunflower oil
650 g/1 lb 7 oz fresh beef mince
1 tbsp tomato purée
1 onion, finely chopped
1 garlic clove, finely chopped
4 tbsp beef stock
salt
soured cream, to serve

method

1 Preheat the oven to 200°C/400°F/Gas Mark 6. Prick the sweet potatoes all over with a fork. Put them directly on an oven shelf and bake in the preheated oven for 1 hour, until soft. When they are cool enough to handle, peel off the skins and chop the flesh.

2 Meanwhile, put the tomatoes, chillies, peppercorns, allspice berries, cinnamon stick and ground coriander into a saucepan and bring to the boil. Reduce the heat and simmer, stirring occasionally, for 30 minutes. Discard the cinnamon stick, then press the sauce through a nylon sieve into a bowl.

3 Heat half the oil in a frying pan. Add the beef and cook over a medium heat, stirring frequently and breaking it up with a wooden spoon, for 8–10 minutes, until evenly browned. Stir in the tomato mixture and tomato purée and season to taste with salt. Simmer, stirring frequently, for 20 minutes.

4 Heat the remaining oil in a frying pan. Add the onion and garlic and cook over a low heat, stirring occasionally, for 5 minutes, until softened. Add the sweet potatoes and stock and cook, stirring constantly, for 5 minutes. Season to taste with salt and transfer to a warmed serving dish. Top with the beef mixture and serve immediately with soured cream.

chilli con carne

ingredients

serves 6

2 tbsp corn oil
2 onions, thinly sliced
2 garlic cloves, finely chopped
650 g/1 lb 7 oz
    fresh beef mince
200 g/7 oz canned chopped
    tomatoes
5 tbsp tomato purée
1 tsp ground cumin
1 tsp cayenne pepper
1 tbsp chilli powder
1 tsp dried oregano
1 bay leaf
350 ml/12 fl oz beef stock
400 g/14 oz canned red kidney
    beans, drained and rinsed
salt
cooked rice, to serve

method

1 Heat the oil in a large saucepan. Add the onions and garlic and cook over a low heat, stirring occasionally, for 5 minutes, until softened. Add the beef, increase the heat to medium and cook, stirring frequently and breaking it up with a wooden spoon, for 8–10 minutes, until evenly browned.

2 Stir in the tomatoes, tomato purée, cumin, cayenne pepper, chilli powder, oregano, bay leaf and stock, then season to taste with salt and bring to the boil. Reduce the heat, cover and simmer, stirring occasionally, for 1 hour.

3 Add the kidney beans, re-cover the pan and simmer, stirring occasionally, for a further 30 minutes. Remove and discard the bay leaf and serve immediately with cooked rice.

small bites & nibbles

dim sum

ingredients

makes 20–24

300 g/10½ oz fresh chicken mince
½ bunch spring onions, trimmed
    and very finely chopped
2 tbsp finely chopped
    fresh coriander
1 tbsp soy sauce
1 tbsp grated fresh ginger
1 tbsp rice wine vinegar
20–24 wonton wrappers
pepper
sweet chilli sauce and dark
    soy sauce, to serve

method

1 Put the mince, spring onions, coriander, soy sauce, ginger and vinegar into a bowl and use a fork to combine. Season to taste with pepper.

2 Place a teaspoon of the prepared filling in the centre of each wonton wrapper. Use your fingers to rub the edges of the wrappers with warm water, gather the 2 opposite edges to form a tight seal, then bring together the remaining 2 sides in the middle at the top.

3 Cover the base of a bamboo steamer with a single layer of the dim sum. Alternatively, line the base of a steamer pan with some baking paper and cover with the dim sum. Place over a saucepan of boiling water, cover and steam for 7–8 minutes.

4 Remove from the steam and serve immediately with the chilli sauce and soy sauce for dipping.

indonesian beef parcels

ingredients

makes 16

4 shallots, finely chopped
2 garlic cloves, finely chopped
500 g/1 lb 2 oz fresh
     beef mince
1 tsp ground cumin
1 tsp ground coriander
2 tsp curry powder
2–3 eggs, lightly beaten
plain flour, for dusting
16 sheets filo pastry
groundnut oil,
     for brushing
salt and pepper

method

1 Put the shallots, garlic, beef, cumin, ground coriander and curry powder into a bowl, then season to taste with salt and pepper and mix well until combined. Heat a wok over a medium heat, then add the beef mixture and cook, stirring constantly, for 8–10 minutes, until the meat is evenly browned. Remove from the heat and leave to cool, then stir in just enough of the beaten egg to bind, reserving the remainder.

2 Preheat the oven to 200°C/400°F/Gas Mark 6. Lightly dust a baking sheet with flour. Brush one sheet of filo with oil, put a second sheet on top and cut the double layer in half. Put a spoonful of the beef mixture in the centre of each piece and fold the sides into the middle. Brush the edges with beaten egg and fold the top and bottom into the middle. Put the parcels on the prepared baking sheet and place in the refrigerator while you make more parcels in the same way.

3 Brush the tops of the parcels with beaten egg and bake in the preheated oven for 20 minutes, until golden brown. Transfer to a warmed serving dish and serve immediately.

aubergine rolls

ingredients

serves 4

100 ml/3½ fl oz olive oil,
    plus extra for brushing
1 onion, grated
1 garlic clove, very finely
    chopped
225 g/8 oz fresh beef mince
2 tomatoes, peeled,
    deseeded and chopped
3 aubergines, peeled and cut into
    5 mm/¼ inch thick slices
6 sheets of filo pastry
salt and pepper

cheese sauce

125 ml/4 fl oz milk
15 g/½ oz butter
15 g/½ oz plain flour
1 egg, lightly beaten
85 g/3 oz Gruyère cheese,
    grated
pinch of ground nutmeg

method

1 Heat 2 tablespoons of the oil in a frying pan. Add the onion and garlic and cook over a low heat, stirring occasionally, for 5 minutes, until softened. Add the beef, increase the heat to medium and cook, stirring frequently and breaking it up with a wooden spoon, for 8–10 minutes, until evenly browned. Pour off the fat then add the tomatoes. Season to taste with salt and pepper and simmer gently for 15–20 minutes. Leave to cool.

2 Meanwhile, make the cheese sauce. Heat the milk, butter and flour in a saucepan, whisking constantly, until smooth and thick. Stir the egg, cheese and nutmeg into the sauce, then stir into the beef mixture.

3 Heat half the remaining oil in a frying pan. Add the aubergine slices and cook for a few minutes on both sides, until golden brown. Drain on kitchen paper.

4 Preheat the oven to 180°C/350°F/Gas Mark 4. Brush a baking sheet with oil. Stack 3 sheets of filo and brush each with oil. Put half the aubergine slices along one long edge, leaving 5 cm/2 inches at each end. Top them with half the beef mixture, spreading it evenly, and roll up the filo. Repeat to make a second roll. Put the rolls onto the prepared baking sheet and brush with the remaining oil. Bake in the preheated oven for 35–40 minutes, until golden brown. Serve immediately.

mini chimichangas

ingredients

makes about 10

2 tbsp vegetable oil, plus extra
   for frying
1 onion, finely chopped
250 g/9 oz fresh chicken mince
1 red chilli, deseeded and
   finely chopped
1 red pepper, deseeded and very
   finely chopped
100 g/3½ oz canned sweetcorn,
   drained
4 spring onions, trimmed and
   finely chopped
4 tbsp fresh tomato salsa
10 small flour tortillas
salt and pepper

method

1 Heat 2 tablespoons of the oil in a non-stick frying pan,
   add the onion and mince and cook for 4–5 minutes,
   until the chicken starts to change colour and the
   onion is soft.

2 Add the chilli and red pepper and cook for a further
   2–3 minutes. Remove from the heat and stir in the
   sweetcorn, spring onions, salsa, and salt and pepper to
   taste and place in a bowl. Wipe out the pan with
   kitchen paper.

3 Warm a tortilla briefly on each side in the pan. Place a
   large spoonful of the filling in the centre, fold in 2 sides
   of the tortilla, then the remaining 2 sides to form a
   small parcel. Secure with a wooden cocktail stick.
   Repeat with the remaining tortillas and filling.

4 Heat enough oil for frying in a frying pan. Add 2–3
   chimichangas and cook for 2 minutes, then turn and
   cook for a further 2–3 minutes, until evenly golden
   brown. Alternatively, heat enough oil for deep-frying in
   a deep-fat fryer to 180–190°C/350–375°F, or until a cube
   of bread browns in 30 seconds. Add 2–3 chimichangas
   and cook for 2–3 minutes, until golden brown. Drain on
   kitchen paper and keep warm while cooking the
   remaining chimichangas. Serve immediately.

beef samosas

ingredients

makes 28

2 tbsp sunflower oil, plus extra
for deep-frying
1 onion, chopped
2 garlic cloves, finely chopped
4-cm/1½-inch piece fresh
ginger, grated
1 tsp chilli powder
1 tsp ground turmeric
1 tsp ground coriander
1 tsp garam masala
500 g/1 lb 2 oz fresh beef
mince
juice of ½ lemon
3 tbsp chopped fresh mint
chilli sauce, to serve

dough

225 g/8 oz plain flour,
plus extra for dusting
large pinch of salt
2 tbsp sunflower oil
about 5 tbsp warm water

method

1 For the dough, sift together the flour and salt into a
bowl. Make a well in the centre and pour in the oil and
water. Gradually incorporate the dry ingredients into the
liquid, adding more water if necessary. Turn out onto a
lightly floured surface and knead until smooth and
elastic. Shape into a ball and leave to rest for 30 minutes.

2 Meanwhile, heat the oil in a large frying pan. Add the
onion, garlic and ginger and cook over a low heat,
stirring occasionally, for 5 minutes, until softened. Stir in
the chilli powder, turmeric, ground coriander and garam
masala and cook, stirring occasionally, for 3 minutes.
Add the beef, increase the heat to medium and cook,
stirring frequently and breaking it up with a wooden
spoon, for 8–10 minutes, until evenly browned. Stir in
the lemon juice and mint and leave to cool.

3 Divide the dough into 14 pieces. Roll out each piece
into an oval about 20 cm/8 inches long. Cut in half
widthways, brush the straight edge with water and fold
in each side to make a cone. Put a tablespoonful of the
beef mixture into each cone, brush the open side with
water and press to seal. Heat enough oil for deep-
frying in a deep-fat fryer to 180–190°C/350–375°F, or
until a cube of bread browns in 30 seconds. Cook the
samosas, in batches, until crisp and golden brown.
Serve with chilli sauce.

beef & pine kernel triangles

ingredients

makes 15

1 tbsp olive oil
1 small onion, chopped
2 garlic cloves, finely chopped
1 tsp ground coriander
1 tsp ground cumin
300 g/10½ oz fresh beef mince
4 tbsp chopped fresh mint
2 tbsp pine kernels
2 potatoes, cut into chunks
55 g/2 oz Kefalotiri or Cheddar
    cheese, grated
115 g/4 oz butter, melted
10 sheets filo pastry
salt
tomato and basil salsa, to serve

method

1 Heat the oil in a large frying pan. Add the onion and
   garlic and cook over a low heat, stirring occasionally, for
   5 minutes, until softened. Stir in the coriander and cumin
   and cook, stirring occasionally, for a further 3 minutes.
   Add the beef, half the mint and the pine kernels.
   Increase the heat to medium and cook, stirring and
   breaking up the meat with a wooden spoon, for 8–10
   minutes, until evenly browned. Season to taste with salt.

2 Meanwhile, cook the potatoes in a saucepan of salted
   boiling water for 15–20 minutes, until tender but not
   falling apart. Drain, tip into a bowl and mash well, then
   stir in the cheese until melted. Stir in the beef mixture.

3 Preheat the oven to 200°C/400°F/Gas Mark 6. Brush 2
   baking sheets with melted butter. Brush 1 sheet of filo
   with melted butter, put a second sheet on top and
   brush with more melted butter. Cut the double layer
   lengthways into 3 strips. Put a heaped tablespoon of
   the filling near 1 end of a strip, then fold over the
   corner to form a triangle. Continue to fold over in
   triangles to make a neat parcel, then place on a
   prepared baking sheet. Make 14 more triangles in the
   same way. Brush with melted butter and bake in the
   preheated oven for 8–10 minutes, until golden brown.
   Serve the pastry triangles with a warm tomato and
   basil salsa.

beef-filled crêpes

ingredients

serves 4

2 tbsp sunflower oil,
    plus extra for brushing
1 onion, chopped
2 carrots, grated
500 g/1 lb 2 oz fresh beef
    mince
1 tbsp tomato purée
1 tbsp plain flour
300 ml/10 fl oz hot beef stock
salt and pepper

crêpe batter

115 g/4 oz plain flour
pinch of salt
1 egg, lightly beaten
300 ml/10 fl oz milk
1 tsp sunflower oil

method

1 First, make the crêpe batter. Sift the flour and salt into a bowl, then add the egg and half the milk and beat until smooth. Stir in the remaining milk and the oil. Set aside.

2 Heat the oil in a frying pan. Add the onion and carrots and cook over a low heat, stirring occasionally, for 5 minutes, until softened. Add the beef, increase the heat to medium and cook, stirring frequently and breaking it up with a wooden spoon, for 8–10 minutes, until evenly browned. Stir the tomato purée and flour into the stock and add to the frying pan. Season to taste with salt and pepper, reduce the heat and simmer, stirring occasionally, for 30 minutes.

3 Meanwhile, brush a crêpe pan with oil and heat. Stir the batter and pour a little into the centre of the pan, then tilt and rotate the pan to cover the base evenly. Cook for 1–1½ minutes, until the underside is golden brown, then flip over the crêpe and cook the other side for 30 seconds. Make more crêpes with the remaining batter, brushing the pan with more oil as required.

4 Preheat the oven to 190°C/375°F/Gas Mark 5. Divide the beef filling between the crêpes and roll them up. Put them into a greased ovenproof dish in a single layer and bake in the preheated oven for 15 minutes. Serve immediately.

beef in pitta pockets

ingredients

serves 4

2 tbsp olive oil
1 onion, chopped
1 garlic clove, chopped
500 g/1 lb 2 oz fresh beef mince
200 g/7 oz canned chopped
   tomatoes
1 tsp ground cumin
1 tsp ground coriander
½ tsp ground turmeric
85 g/3 oz pine kernels
2 tbsp chopped fresh coriander
salt and pepper

to serve

8 pitta breads, warmed
chopped cucumber
shredded lettuce
soured cream

method

1 Heat the oil in a frying pan. Add the onion and garlic and cook over a low heat, stirring occasionally, for 5 minutes, until softened. Add the beef, increase the heat to medium and cook, stirring frequently and breaking it up with a wooden spoon, for 8–10 minutes, until evenly browned. Stir in the tomatoes, cumin, ground coriander and turmeric. Season to taste with salt and pepper, reduce the heat and simmer, stirring occasionally, for 15–20 minutes.

2 Meanwhile, dry-fry the pine kernels in a small frying pan, stirring constantly, until golden. Stir the pine kernels and chopped coriander into the meat mixture and simmer for 3–4 minutes.

3 To serve, cut a slit in the side of each pitta bread to make a pocket. Put a little of the beef mixture into each pocket with some chopped cucumber and shredded lettuce. Top with a spoonful of soured cream and serve immediately.

curry puffs

ingredients

makes 20

2 tbsp groundnut oil
1 onion, finely chopped
1 garlic clove, finely chopped
1-cm/½-inch piece fresh ginger,
    finely chopped
2 fresh red chillies, deseeded and
    finely chopped
1 tsp chilli powder
½ tsp ground coriander
½ tsp ground turmeric
225 g/8 oz fresh beef mince
1 tomato, peeled and diced
55 g/2 oz frozen peas, thawed
2 tbsp lime juice
500 g/1 lb 2 oz ready-made puff
    pastry, thawed if frozen
plain flour, for dusting
1 egg, lightly beaten
salt

method

1 Heat the oil in a frying pan. Add the onion, garlic, ginger and chillies and cook over a low heat, stirring occasionally, for 5 minutes, until softened. Stir in the chilli powder, ground coriander and turmeric, season to taste with salt and cook, stirring occasionally, for a further 3 minutes.

2 Add the beef, increase the heat to medium and cook, stirring frequently and breaking it up with a wooden spoon, for 8–10 minutes, until evenly browned. Stir in the tomato, peas and lime juice, reduce the heat and cook, stirring occasionally, for a further 5 minutes. Remove the pan from the heat

3 Preheat the oven to 200°C/400°F/Gas Mark 6. Roll out the pastry on a lightly floured surface to a thickness of about 3 mm/⅛ inch. Stamp out 20 rounds with a 10-cm/4-inch pastry cutter. Put 2 teaspoons of the beef mixture to the side of each round. Brush the edges with water and fold over, pressing the edges to seal. Crimp the edges with a fork. Put the puffs on a baking sheet, brush with the beaten egg and bake in the preheated oven for 20–30 minutes, until golden brown.

4 Remove from the oven, transfer to a wire rack and leave to cool slightly. Serve warm.

beef & onion piroshki

ingredients

makes 40–45

55 g/2 oz butter, plus extra
    for greasing
1 onion, finely chopped
225 g/8 oz fresh beef mince
55 g/2 oz cooked rice
2 tbsp soured cream
1 tsp Worcestershire sauce
1 tsp caraway seeds
1 hard-boiled egg, chopped
1 egg, beaten with 1 tsp water
salt and pepper

dough

350 g/12 oz plain flour,
    plus extra for dusting
pinch of salt
55 g/2 oz cream cheese
115 g/4 oz butter
about 3 tbsp water
3 tbsp double cream

method

1 For the dough, sift the flour and salt into a bowl. Add the cream cheese and butter and rub in with your fingertips until the mixture resembles breadcrumbs. Add the water and cream 1 tablespoon at a time. Knead gently, adding more water if necessary. Shape into a ball, cover and chill in the refrigerator for 30 minutes.

2 Meanwhile, melt the butter in a saucepan. Add the onion and cook over a low heat, stirring occasionally, for 5 minutes, until softened. Add the beef, increase the heat to medium and cook, stirring frequently and breaking it up with a wooden spoon, for 8–10 minutes, until evenly browned. Remove the pan from the heat, stir in the rice, soured cream, Worcestershire sauce, caraway seeds and chopped egg and season to taste with salt and pepper.

3 Preheat the oven to 200°C/400°F/Gas Mark 6. Grease 2 baking sheets with butter. Roll out the dough to a thickness of about 3 mm/⅛ inch on a lightly floured surface. Stamp out rounds with an 8-cm/3¼-inch plain cutter. Put a teaspoon of the filling on each round. Brush the edges of the rounds with beaten egg, then fold the dough over. Press the edges to seal and crimp with a fork. Place on the prepared baking sheets and brush with beaten egg. Bake in the preheated oven for 20 minutes, until golden brown. Serve immediately.

rissoles

ingredients

serves 6

1 kg/2 lb 4 oz potatoes, cut
    into chunks
1 onion, finely chopped
500 g/1 lb 2 oz fresh beef
    mince
1 tbsp snipped fresh chives
1 tbsp chopped fresh parsley
2 tsp Worcestershire sauce or
    tomato ketchup
3 eggs
3 tbsp plain flour
175 g/6 oz fresh breadcrumbs
sunflower oil, for shallow-frying
salt and pepper

method

1 Cook the potatoes in a large saucepan of salted boiling water for 20–25 minutes, until tender but not falling apart. Drain well, tip into a bowl and mash the potatoes until smooth.

2 Add the onion, beef, chives, parsley and Worcestershire sauce and season to taste with salt and pepper. Mix well until thoroughly combined. Cover the bowl with clingfilm and chill the mixture in the refrigerator for 30–45 minutes to firm up.

3 Dampen your hands and shape the mixture into 12 sausage-shaped rissoles. Lightly beat the eggs in a shallow dish, spread out the flour in a second shallow dish and spread out the breadcrumbs in a third shallow dish.

4 Pour oil into a large frying pan to a depth of about 1 cm/½ inch and heat. Meanwhile, coat the rissoles first in the flour, then in the beaten egg and, finally, in the breadcrumbs. Shake off any excess.

5 Add the rissoles to the frying pan, in batches if necessary, and cook over a medium heat, turning occasionally, for 8–10 minutes, until crisp, evenly browned and cooked through. Remove from the pan with a fish slice and keep warm while you cook the remaining rissoles. Serve immediately.

albondigas (spanish meatballs)

ingredients

serves 4–6

500 g/1 lb 2 oz fresh beef mince
85 g/3 oz long-grain rice, cooked, cooled and chilled
1 onion, finely chopped
1 garlic clove, crushed
1 egg, beaten
3 tbsp finely chopped fresh flat-leaf parsley
vegetable oil, for frying
salt and pepper
pitta breads and salad leaves, to serve

method

1 Put the mince, rice, onion, garlic, egg and parsley into a bowl and use your fingertips to combine. Season to taste with salt and pepper. Shape the mixture into 18–20 small meatballs, place on a baking tray, cover and chill for 20–30 minutes.

2 Heat the oil in a frying pan, add the meatballs in 2 batches and cook, turning regularly, for about 12–14 minutes, until thoroughly cooked.

3 Serve in pitta breads with salad leaves.

beef & mozzarella risotto balls

ingredients

serves 4

300 g/10½ oz long-grain rice
55 g/2 oz butter
2 tbsp grated Parmesan cheese
1 tbsp chopped fresh parsley
1 tbsp olive oil
1 shallot, finely chopped
1 garlic clove, finely chopped
115 g/4 oz fresh beef mince
100 ml/3½ fl oz dry white wine
2 tbsp tomato purée
115 g/4 oz mozzarella cheese,
    cut into cubes
2 eggs
55 g/2 oz plain flour
sunflower oil, for deep-frying
salt and pepper

method

1 Cook the rice in a large saucepan of salted boiling water for 15 minutes, until tender. Drain, rinse with boiling water and return to the pan. Stir in half the butter, the Parmesan and parsley. Spread out on a baking sheet and leave to cool.

2 Meanwhile, melt the remaining butter with the olive oil in a saucepan. Add the shallot and garlic and cook over a low heat, stirring occasionally, for 5 minutes, until softened. Add the beef, increase the heat to medium and cook, stirring frequently and breaking it up with a wooden spoon, for 5–8 minutes, until evenly browned. Stir in the wine and cook for 5 minutes. Reduce the heat and stir in the tomato purée, then cover and simmer for 15 minutes. Season to taste with salt and pepper.

3 When the rice is cold, shape into balls. Make a small hollow in each and put a spoonful of meat mixture and a cube of cheese inside, then re-shape to enclose the filling. Lightly beat the eggs in a dish and spread out the flour in a separate dish. Dip the balls in the egg and then in the flour. Heat enough sunflower oil for deep-frying in a deep-fat fryer to 180–190°C/350–375°F, or until a cube of bread browns in 30 seconds. Cook the balls, in batches, until golden brown, and serve immediately.

beef & herb croquettes

ingredients

serves 6

2 tbsp sunflower oil
1 Spanish onion,
  finely chopped
2 garlic cloves, finely chopped
1 kg/2 lb 4 oz fresh
  beef mince
3 eggs
2 tbsp soured cream
1 tbsp chopped fresh flat-leaf
  parsley, plus extra sprigs
  to garnish
1 tsp sweet paprika
115 g/4 oz fresh breadcrumbs
85 g/3 oz butter
salt and pepper

method

1 Heat the oil in a frying pan. Add the onion and garlic
   and cook over a low heat, stirring occasionally, for
   8–10 minutes, until golden brown.

2 Transfer the onion and garlic to a large bowl, add the
   beef, one of the eggs, the soured cream, chopped
   parsley, paprika and 25 g/1 oz of the breadcrumbs and
   season to taste with salt and pepper. Using your hands,
   mix well until all the ingredients are thoroughly
   combined. Shape the mixture into 12 croquettes.

3 Lightly beat the remaining eggs in a shallow dish and
   spread out the remaining breadcrumbs in a separate
   shallow dish. Coat the croquettes first in beaten egg
   and then in breadcrumbs.

4 Melt the butter in a large frying pan. Add the
   croquettes, in batches if necessary, and cook over a
   medium heat for 5–6 minutes on each side, until
   evenly browned and cooked through. Remove from
   the pan with a fish slice and keep warm while you cook
   the remaining croquettes. Garnish with parsley sprigs
   and serve immediately.

indian potato cakes

ingredients

makes 10

1 kg/2 lb 4 oz potatoes,
    cut into chunks
100 ml/3½ fl oz groundnut oil
1 large onion, finely chopped
2 garlic cloves, finely chopped
2 fresh green chillies, deseeded
    and finely chopped
4-cm/1½-inch piece fresh
    ginger, finely chopped
1 tsp ground cumin
1 tsp ground coriander
2 tbsp chopped fresh mint
1 tbsp chopped fresh coriander
225 g/8 oz fresh beef mince
55 g/2 oz frozen peas, thawed
4 tbsp lemon juice
2 eggs
115 g/4 oz fresh breadcrumbs
salt

method

1 Cook the potatoes in a large saucepan of salted boiling water for 20–25 minutes, until tender but not falling apart. Drain, return to the pan and mash well.

2 Heat 1 tablespoon of the oil in a large frying pan. Add the onion, garlic, chillies, ginger, cumin, ground coriander, mint and chopped coriander and cook over a low heat, stirring occasionally, for 5 minutes. Add the beef, increase the heat to medium and cook, stirring frequently and breaking it up with a wooden spoon, for 5 minutes. Add the peas and cook, stirring frequently, for a further 3–5 minutes, until the meat is evenly browned and the mixture is dry. Remove from the heat, season to taste with salt and stir in the lemon juice.

3 Divide the mashed potato into 10 portions. Put one portion in your hand and flatten it into a round. Put a spoonful of the beef mixture in the middle and re-shape to enclose the filling. Make 9 more in the same way.

4 Lightly beat the eggs in a shallow dish. Spread out the breadcrumbs in a separate shallow dish. Dip the potato cakes in the beaten egg and then in the breadcrumbs to coat. Chill in the refrigerator for 30 minutes.

5 Heat the remaining oil in a frying pan. Add the potato cakes, in batches, and cook over a medium heat, turning occasionally, until golden brown. Serve immediately.

fried beef dumplings with tomato sauce

ingredients

serves 6

650 g/1 lb 7 oz fresh beef mince
250 g/9 oz shredded beef suet
4½ tbsp finely chopped onion
½ tsp ground ginger
¼ tsp ground cloves
¼ tsp ground nutmeg
1 large egg, lightly beaten
85 g/3 oz medium oatmeal
vegetable oil, for deep-frying
salt and pepper

tomato sauce

2 tbsp sunflower oil
1 onion, finely chopped
2 garlic cloves, finely chopped
2 tbsp tomato purée
100 ml/3½ fl oz water
400 g/14 oz canned chopped
   tomatoes

method

1 First, make the tomato sauce. Heat the oil in a saucepan, add the onion and garlic and cook over a low heat, stirring occasionally, for 5 minutes, until softened. Add the tomato purée, water and tomatoes and bring to the boil then simmer for 15–20 minutes.

2 Put the beef, suet and onion into a bowl and mix well. Add the spices, season to taste with salt and pepper and mix well again. Finally, add the egg and mix until thoroughly combined.

3 Break off pieces of the mixture and shape into 5-cm/2-inch balls. Spread out the oatmeal in a shallow dish and roll the dumplings in it until coated.

4 Heat enough oil for deep-frying in a deep-fat fryer to 180–190°C/350–375°F, or until a cube of bread browns in 30 seconds. Add the dumplings and cook for 8–10 minutes, until golden brown and cooked through.

5 Remove the dumplings and drain well. Transfer to a warmed serving dish and serve immediately with the tomato sauce.

crispy beef fritters

ingredients

serves 4

4 eggs, separated
225 g/8 oz fresh beef mince
1 small onion, very finely chopped
½ tsp baking powder
2 tbsp chopped fresh parsley
1 tbsp Worcestershire sauce
4 tbsp sunflower oil
salt and pepper

method

1 Beat the egg yolks in a large bowl until pale and thick. Fold in the beef, onion, baking powder, parsley and Worcestershire sauce and season to taste with salt and pepper. Stir gently until thoroughly combined.

2 Whisk the egg whites in a separate grease-free bowl until stiff, then gently fold them into the beef mixture.

3 Heat the oil in a large frying pan. Drop tablespoonfuls of the beef mixture, about 4 at a time, into the hot oil and fry for 3 minutes, or until puffed up and brown at the edges. Using a spatula or slotted spoon, turn the fritters over and fry for a further 2–3 minutes.

4 Remove with a slotted spoon and drain on kitchen paper. Keep warm while you cook the remaining fritters, then serve immediately.

stuffed beef rolls

ingredients

serves 4

175 g/6 oz fresh beef mince
1 shallot, finely chopped
25 g/1 oz butter
25 g/1 oz fresh breadcrumbs
grated rind of 1 lemon
6 green olives,
    stoned and chopped
1 egg, lightly beaten
8 slices topside of beef, each
    about 5 mm/¼ inch thick
2 tbsp olive oil
2 onions, finely chopped
1 garlic clove, finely chopped
2 carrots, finely chopped
300 ml/10 fl oz beef stock
2 tomatoes, peeled,
    deseeded and sliced
1 bay leaf
3 tbsp finely chopped
    fresh parsley
salt and pepper

method

1 Preheat the oven to 180°C/350°F/Gas Mark 4. Put the beef mince, shallot, butter, breadcrumbs, lemon rind and olives into a bowl and mix well. Add the egg, then season to taste with salt and pepper and mix until thoroughly combined. Divide the mixture between the beef slices, then roll up and tie with kitchen string.

2 Heat the oil in a flameproof casserole. Add the beef rolls, in batches, and cook over a low–medium heat, turning occasionally, until browned all over. Remove with a slotted spoon and set aside.

3 Add the onions, garlic and carrots to the casserole and cook over a low heat, stirring occasionally, for 5 minutes. Add the stock, tomatoes and bay leaf and bring to the boil. Remove the casserole from the heat and return the beef rolls to it, then cover and cook in the preheated oven for 1½ hours.

4 Remove the casserole from the oven and lift out the beef rolls. Carefully remove and discard the string and put the rolls on a warmed serving plate. Strain the cooking liquid into a jug, pressing down on the vegetables with the back of a spoon. Taste and adjust the seasoning, adding salt and pepper if needed, then pour the sauce over the beef rolls. Sprinkle with the parsley and serve immediately.

meatballs on sticks

ingredients

serves 6–8

4 pork and herb sausages
115 g/4 oz fresh beef mince
85 g/3 oz fresh white breadcrumbs
1 onion, finely chopped
1 tsp finely chopped parsley
1 tsp finely chopped thyme
1 tsp finely chopped sage
1 egg
sunflower oil, for greasing
salt and pepper

method

1 Preheat the grill to medium–high, or alternatively preheat the barbecue. Remove the sausage meat from the skins, place in a large bowl and break up with a fork. Add the beef mince, breadcrumbs, onion, herbs and egg. Season to taste with salt and pepper and stir well with a wooden spoon until thoroughly mixed.

2 Form the mixture into small balls, about the size of a golf ball, between the palms of your hands. Spear each meatball with a cocktail stick and brush with oil.

3 Cook under the preheated grill, or over medium–hot coals, turning frequently and brushing with more oil as necessary, for 10 minutes, or until cooked through. Serve immediately.

index